TEXT: **Ann McCarthy**

CAPTIONS: **Pauline Graham**

DESIGNED BY: **Teddy Hartshorn**

EDITORIAL: **Gill Waugh and Pauline Graham**

PRODUCTION: **Ruth Arthur and David Proffit**

DIRECTOR OF PRODUCTION: **Gerald Hughes**

DIRECTOR OF PUBLISHING: **David Gibbon**

CLB 2447
© 1990 Colour Library Books Ltd., Godalming, Surrey, England.
All rights reserved.
This 1990 edition is published by Crescent Books,
distributed by Outlet Book Company, Inc., a Random House Company,
40 Engelhard Avenue, Avenel, New Jersey 07001.

Random House
New York • Toronto • London • Sydney • Auckland

Printed and bound in Singapore

ISBN 0-517-00177-2

10 9 8 7 6 5

MINNESOTA

A Photographic Journey

Text by
ANN McCARTHY

CRESCENT BOOKS
NEW YORK · AVENEL, NEW JERSEY

Far up on the North Shore of Lake Superior, near the tip of Minnesota's Arrowhead Country, lies the Indian village of Grand Portage. To reach it by land you must wind your way down a narrow dirt road to a small bay on the lake shore. In the 1790s it was the busiest, most exciting place in all of Minnesota. This now deserted fur trading post was the doorway to riches.

Once, vast fortunes in furs went through it, the gold of the Northwest, for which men risked their lives winter after dreary winter in the wilderness west of Lake Superior. In George Washington's time the name Grand Portage, a mere spot in an untamed land, was known in Europe, while St. Paul and Chicago were not even listed on the map. That was long before Minnesota became a part of the United States or was settled at all.

"Grand Portage" or "the great carrying place," got its name because the falls and rapids in the Pigeon River made it necessary to carry canoes and supplies overland to Lake Superior. The trail was nine miles long, the second-longest portage on the entire route from Montreal to the Rockies. The flags of Great Britain, France and the United States have waved over it. Until 1762 it was used largely by the French, then the British and, finally, as a result of the War of 1812, by the United States.

The fur trading post on Lake Superior was a meeting place for men from the North West Company, the Hudson's Bay Company, the XY Company and John Jacob Astor's American Fur Company. From 1783 until 1803 it was considered this country's greatest fur depot. Daniel Harmon, a partner in the North West Company, visited Grand Portage for the first time in June, 1800. He wrote in his journal: 'Within the fort, there is a considerable number of dwelling houses, shops and stores ... The houses are surrounded by palisades ... sunk nearly three feet in the ground and rise about fifteen feet above it ... This is the Head Quarters for all who trade in this part of the world; and therefore, every summer, the greater part (of the men) who have spent the winter in the Interior come here with the furs which they have been able to collect, during the preceding season ... The people who come from Montreal with the goods ... on their return take down the furs etc.. from the north."

The men who spent their winters in the wilds north and west of Grand Portage were known as "winterers" or "Nor'westers." They looked down on the "pork-eaters", men who came from Montreal to Grand Portage and ventured no further. The pork-eaters brought guns, trade goods, blankets, knives and other supplies from Montreal and took back the pelts of beaver, muskrat, marten, mink and racoon. The pork-eaters' canoe was large and took from ten to fourteen men to paddle, while the canoe used by the Nor-westers was smaller, lighter and better suited to the inland lakes.

The pork-eaters didn't just surreptitiously slip into Grand Portage each summer. Grace Lee Nute wrote: "Before Hat Point was turned, these voyageurs must prepare for the grand flourish with which every canoe was expected to enter the bay and approach the fort. On some rocky point the men doffed their workaday clothes and donned the colourful dress of voyageurs ... The bright sash that encircled the waist several times ... and the great capote, whose hood was a boon when clouds of mosquitoes attacked the hard-working paddlers or when snow squalls made them shiver. Bathed, shaven, and tricked out in holiday dress, the voyageurs entered their canoes once more and came up the bay swinging red-bladed paddles, a stroke every second, and chanting one of their canoe songs."

The great hall at Grand Portage was the scene of much merriment and fighting. On July 4, 1800, Daniel Harmon described the day's activities: "In the daytime the (Indians) were permitted to dance in the fort, ... In the evening the gentlemen of the place dressed and we had a famous ball in the dining room. For musick, we had the bag-pipe, the violin and the flute." The men had Indian maidens for dancing partners, and Harmon was surprised that they conducted themselves "with so much propriety and danced so well." The feasts consisted of "bread, salt pork, beef, hams, fish and venison, butter, peas, Indian corn, potatoes, tea, spirits, wine, etc., and plenty of milk."

The North West Company and the others eventually moved to Fort Williams. A port remained at Grand Portage until after the War of 1812, but weeds grew up over the trail and fort. The days of glory for the frontier trading metropolis were over.

Grand Portage, part of the Arrowhead region in northeastern Minnesota, rims the world's largest freshwater lake, Lake Superior. In Duluth, from the famous Aerial Lift Bridge, visitors watch giant ships wave the flags of dozens of nations as they enter the Lake Superior port. Mines have also brought fame to the Arrowhead region. The world's largest open-pit iron ore mine is in Hibbing. Way up north, almost to the Canadian border, is International Falls, called the "ice box of the nation." International Falls' sub-zero temperatures are often quoted in Florida, to entice vacationers to stay longer. The frigid city is located on the south bank of Rainy River. Rainy Lake, with its 3,500 miles of shoreline and more than 3,000 islands, is just north of the city.

The United States Hockey Hall of Fame is in Eveleth; Ely is the gateway to the federally protected Boundary Waters Canoe Area wilderness (BWCA), and the fifty-eight-mile Gunflint Trail starts in Grand Marais and weaves through Superior National Forest. Northeast of Grand Marais lies the Grand Portage National Monument, an authentic reconstruction of the North West Company Stockade trading post established in 1778. The Arrowhead region contains more than twenty of Minnesota's sixty-four state parks and the state's only national park, Voyageurs National Park, which contains the state's largest Indian Burial Mounds. Lutsen downhill ski area, on the North Shore of Lake Superior, is appreciated for its beauty and 700-foot vertical drop. Towering above the beaches south of Lutsen stands the famous Split Rock Lighthouse.

At the edge of Lake Superior are cascading waterfalls, high rock bluffs, long stretches of beach set with precious agates and original driftwood artworks. Behind the beaches are lush, enveloping woods which hold rivers gently tumbling over rocks or rushing ferociously over falls. Foot bridges link the river banks and red bunchberries, pearly everlastings, daisy asters, lacy ferns, ancient, exposed gnarled roots, and freckled, bright orange mushrooms decorate the spongy, moss-layered forest floor. Flecks of sunlight sneak through and spotlight vegetation. The huge hideaway is a place to establish a rapport with nature. One feels both protected and free when surrounded by the fresh, green smells and the animated sounds of the woodland.

Beyond the thick, protecting woods lies the mysterious and majestic, seemingly endless expanse of Lake Superior. An occasional island dots the surface between land and horizon, where a lone barge breaks the line where the water meets the sky.

Lake Superior plunges to more than a quarter-mile at its deepest and covers 31,820 square miles – an area equivalent to half of New England. Something like two hundred rivers, fed by more than 1,200 tributaries, course their waters into its vast bowl. The water is tea-colored, dyed with tannic acid from the dead vegetation that blankets the woods in which these rivers rise. Virtually every drop of water poured into Lake Superior will find its way to the sea, 2,300 miles away. Much of that journey is through the 1,200-mile chain of the four other Great Lakes – Michigan, Huron, Erie and Ontario, and then through the St. Lawrence Seaway.

Despite the damage twentieth century pollution has generated in the other Great Lakes and the taconite tailings near Duluth, Lake Superior is, for the most part "in a pristine state not far removed from the composition of rainwater." The ageing of a lake depends on climate, its size, depth and chemical makeup, the mineral content of its surrounding drainage basin and man. Superior has been allowed to stay young largely because of its isolation. When the other lakes were bustling, Superior remained remote. Even after a canal through Sault Ste. Marie opened in 1855 and allowed inland commerce, it was considered a "separate and foreign country, far removed from the 'real' United States." Walter Havighurst wrote in *The Great Lakes Reader*: "Until the 1890s post offices beyond the Soo were addressed LS. (Lake Superior), the newspapers were dated that way, and a man going from Duluth or Marquette to Chicago, Detroit, or Cleveland spoke of 'returning to the United States.' The North was a back-of-beyond country, and a luring one, like Alaska in the twentieth century."

The remoteness and vastness of the lake lent it an aura of mystery which incited legends and literature. Longfellow's "Song of Hiawatha" is the most celebrated Lake Superior poem. Though the tale of this warrior has been traced to the Algonquin tribe in New York State, Longfellow declared categorically: "The scene of the poem is among the Ojibways (Chippewa) on the southern shore of Lake Superior, in the region between the Pictured Rocks and the Grand Sable." Written in classic form modeled on a melancholy Finnish epic, "The Song of Hiawatha" faithfully renders the blend of romance and fear with which the Indians had viewed the Big Sea Water for centuries:

> "By the shores of Gitche Gumee,
> By the shining Big Sea Water,
> Stood the wigwam of Nokomis,
> Daughter of the Moon, Nokomis.
> Dark behind it rose the forest,
> Rose the black and gloomy pine trees,
> Rose the firs with cones upon them;
> Bright before it beat the water,
> Beat the clear and sunny water,
> Beat the shining Big Sea Water."

But this vast lake is an unforgiving environment, a perilous realm where shipwrecks have prevailed.

Winds build up tremendous force over the miles of open water. They whip up "steep, sharp-edged waves that create a violent chop." On November 27-28, 1905, snow began to fall and winds rose quickly to a howl, reaching the near-hurricane force of seventy-nine miles an hour. It became a nightmare storm, with eighteen ships disabled or destroyed and five men killed.

The most bizarre wreck, which came to be known as the "Blow of '5," occurred within shouting distance of the main street of Duluth – within sight of thousands of spectators, plus a thwarted crew of United States Life Savers. The 430-foot steamer *Mataafa* had weathered the death-defying waters of the night of the twenty-seventh, and the captain had ordered her back to Duluth after daybreak on the twenty-eighth. In zero visibility and mountainous waves, the ship moved slowly toward port. About noon the snow lightened a bit and the captain saw the narrow, rocky harbor entrance. He waited for the right time, then slammed ahead at full steam. Just as he got to the entrance, a massive wave swelled beneath the stern and lifted it so high that the ship's bow was smashed downward into the lake bottom. Another wave struck her midships, shoving her sideways against the stone piers. Her engines became water-logged as the *Mataafa* lay trapped against the pier. Wave after wave smashed into her until, at last, the hull broke in two. The *Mataafa's* decks were awash with frothing water as three of the twelve men aft dashed to join the twelve in the bow, where there was some small shelter in the pilothouse. Nine remained trapped on the stern. The meager protection there was provided by the smokestack and ventilator hoods.

Through the night several thousand Duluthians lined the beach and waited by bonfires for the storm to subside so they could rescue the desperate men. They would be too late for some of them. In a book called *Memories of the Lakes*, Dana Thomas Bowen recalled: "Nine men perished in the after end, due to exposure. The fires under her boilers had been extinguished as the stern settled, leaving the men without heat. Reports tell of finding the men encased in ice in the after end. Some had sought shelter in the ventilator hoods and had to be chopped free. One engineer was encased in ice behind the stack."

The fifteen men in the pilot house did survive the night. Professor Julius F. Wolff Jr. of the University of Minnesota at Duluth wrote: "They collected all of the Ship's lamps in the forepeak, those being lighted for heat. The captain instructed the mates and wheelmen to keep the men on their feet and moving even though all were already worn out. As the temperature dropped toward morning, the captain eventually got a bonfire started in the windlass room ... the fire kept all from freezing to death. With the wind and seas dropping at daybreak, the Life Savers returned with a surfboat. In a death-defying launch through still mountainous surf they quickly reached the *Mataafa* and in two trips removed the fifteen crewmen left alive."

Through the centuries several ships have simply disappeared on the Great Lakes. The most recent and memorable murder mystery on Lake Superior happened on November 10, 1975. On this day the *Edmund Fitzgerald*, a 729-foot ore carrier known as "Big Fitz" because it was the biggest of its kind in the world when launched in 1958, was headed east on the lake. She had left Duluth in balmy Indian summer weather. But the shining Big Sea Water is fickle. Within twenty four hours the "Fitz" was in battle with a wrathful storm and losing. The unofficial wind velocity went as high as ninety miles per hour, and the waves were estimated to be as high as thirty feet.

The *Fitzgerald's* skipper radioed the *Arthur M. Anderson*, the nearest ship, and said that his radar had stopped working and asked to be kept in sight. Toward evening the captain of the *Fitzgerald* reported over his radio, "We're in a big sea. I've never seen anything like it in my life."

At 7:10 p.m., the second day out, the *Fitzgerald* was still visible on the Anderson's radar scope. The first mate radioed the *Fitzgerald* to ask how she was doing. "We're holding our own," the captain said calmly. Between intermittent snow storms, the crew of the *Anderson* could see the running lights of the other ship.

A sudden snow squall diminished visibility to zero. It lasted five minutes, then cleared. The crew of the *Anderson* was numb - the *Fitzgerald* was no longer there. They could see the lights of other ships in the distance, but the *Fitzgerald* was gone. She had vanished and twenty-nine men went with her. No trace of them was ever found.

Because of Lake Superior's purity the bodies would be preserved and not rise to the surface. The Big Sea Water had claimed another cache of victims who disappeared without a definite explanation.

The city most associated with Lake Superior is Duluth, Minnesota's third largest metropolis. Mark Twain once said, "The coldest winter I ever spent was summer in Duluth." But John Guntheer writing in *Inside U.S.A.*, in 1947, gave the city a more favorable report:

"There is more to Minnesota than just politics, Stassen and the Twin Cities. Consider merely what Sinclair Lewis calls the radiant, sea-fronting, hillside city of Duluth. I drove up to Duluth from Minneapolis, and in fact it was Mr. Lewis who was my host there. We looked at what is called Minnesota Point from a tall bluff, and watched the freighters come in with coal, and go out again with their mammoth burdens of ore, against the swelling blue backdrop of Lake Superior. Duluth is the end of the line. Here is the extreme westernmost tip of the Atlantic Ocean. Duluth, together with Superior (Wisconsin), is a seaport, though its shining water is fresh, not salt. But it is difficult, up in this piney stillness, to appreciate the well-known fact that this is the second largest port in the nation; there is something incongruous about its commercial activity. 'Port' connotes smoke and slums and men hurrying down greasy, cobbled streets, whereas Duluth tingles with openness, the atmospshere of campfires, placid sunshine, and the free spirit of the Viking north."

Minnesotans connect Duluth with Lake Superior. They also know that somewhere near Duluth is "The Range."

The discovery of the Vermilion Range in the 1880s and the Mesabi in the 1890s caused a boom unprecedented in the history of Minnesota's frontier. Though few would have expected it, the Mesabi Range became the largest iron-ore producer in the nation. Iron-seeking businesses were attracted to the territory and they sent representatives to settle around the new source of wealth. In just a few years straggling camps like Tower, Ely, Virginia, Hibbing, Mountain Iron and Chisholm became small cities, and Duluth, the emporium of an impressive mining and lumbering region, rapidly developed into a mini-metropolis.

Valuable minerals have been found near the shores of Lake Superior for centuries. About 1,000 B.C. Indians devised a way to mine copper in the area. Much later, in 1826, Lewis Cass reserved mineral rights in Northern Minnesota through a treaty with the Chippewa, even though there was no sign of copper or iron.

Then Daniel Webster, writing under the authority of President John Tyler, stated that the region between the Pigeon and St. Louis rivers, later known as the Arrowhead Region, had superior mineral deposits. Although Webster was propagandizing, he proved to have foresight when the United States Geological Survey team reported the discovery of iron ore near Arrowhead's Gunflint Lake in 1850.

The find caused Governor Alexander Ramsey to engage in further investigation of the territory's mineral prospects. What Richard Eaves found brought on mild hysteria – mineral-bearing quartz, which the chief assayer of the federal mint in Philadelphia determined would yield $25.63 in gold and $4.42 in silver to the short ton. The Vermilion Lake Gold Rush of 1865-1866 was on. As the expectant beat a path to the potential source of their riches, a wagon road was opened to Duluth, and Lake Vermilion developed all the trappings of a California gold rush town. Everything was there but the gold. The rush was a bust, but the area was open to more geological exploration.

Lewis Merritt, a veteran timber cruiser, insisted that the Mesabi held iron ore. He passed his business on to his four sons and told them and their three cousins to keep one eye on the ground while they were surveying lumber. The Merritt brothers were camped in the stony Mesabi hills when, under a thick floor of pine, they inadvertantly discovered a powdery red substance. It was not hard like other iron ore, but testing in Duluth proved that it contained 64 percent iron. The Merritt's next concern was how to transport the ore. They built a railroad line which would join the established Duluth and Winnipeg Railroad at Brookston, about twenty-five miles west of Duluth. In October of 1892, the Merritts sent their first shipment from Mountain Iron to Superior, Wisconsin, and on through the Great Lakes to the steel mills in Cleveland, Pittsburg and Buffalo. But the Duluth and Winnipeg Railroad failed to come through with the promised ore cars.

The Merritts persuaded John D. Rockefeller to bail them out of their financial difficulties. Not without stipulations, however. Andrew Carnegie, Jay Cooke and Henry Frick also bought or leased Mesabi lands. When the Oliver-Frick-Carnegie interests were merged in 1901 into United States Steel, a coalition engineered by J.P Morgan, Minnesota's iron-bearing lands passed almost entirely into the Oliver Division of the mammoth corporation. A total of 400 mines on Minnesota's three iron ranges (Vermillion, Mesabi and Cuyana) produced the ore which supplied most of growing America's demand for steel.

The people who were drawn to the Mesabi mines represented a potpourri of immigrant groups. In the first influx were Englishmen, Scotsmen, Irishmen, French-Canadians, Scandinavians, Finns, Slovenes, Italians, Bohemians, Poles and Lithuanians, as well as Yankees. After 1900, Slavs and Latins began to arrive in substantial numbers. They included Greeks, Croats, Serbs,

Montenegrins, Bulgarians, Russians and others. By 1910, there were at least thirty-five minority groups of sufficient size to be identified. The diverse immigrant groups who settled on the range and worked in the mines enriched the heritage of northern Minnesota.

Hinckley sits at the southernmost point of the Arrowhead area. In the mid-1800s pine was king and Hinkley was in the middle of pine country. But the summer of 1894 was dry and hot throughout the Mississippi and Missouri River valleys. Fires had flared all summer in the forested regions of Northern Minnesota, Wisconsin and Michigan. The skies over the Great Lakes were misted with smoke, at times causing hazardous shipping conditions. On July 18 and 19 *The Duluth News Tribune* reported that fires were burning along St. Paul and Duluth tracks from Pine City to Carlton and threatening Hinckley. The paper also noted that temperatures at Duluth in mid-July had exceeded ninety degrees for several days. On July 25 Mankato reported a temperature of 102 degrees and Faribault, 108 degrees.

Saturday, September 1, began in Hinckley with the usual blast from the Brennan Lumber Company whistle at 7 a.m. It signalled the beginning of the ten-hour day shift which would turn out 200,000 feet of lumber to be added to the tidy piles of twenty-eight million feet in the yards. For days the sunsets had been redder than normal and a yellow haze hovered over the town. The smell of smoke and dust commingled. All summer the villagers had fought off approaching fires, feeling confident that the rains would come soon. Besides, in 1892 the nineteen-man Hinckley volunteer fire department had won second place in a fire fighting contest between all fire departments west of Chicago. They had snappy new uniforms and a new fire engine with its own hot water boiler and steam-driven pistons which produced greater pressure than former models. The fire department would be able to hold off any real trouble. Throughout the morning the air seemed oppressively still and heavy and the sun had turned an ominous red. Toward noon the wind began to stiffen, sifting ashes and cinders in the air. Sometime between one and two p.m. the fire alarm sounded its shrill warning. Thick, grey smoke flowed in, then briefly lifted leaving a yellow shroud over the town. Before long dense ashes and smoke blanketed Hinckley again and a blackened sky hovered overhead. The people began to abandon their homes. But Thomas Dunn, a twenty-five-year-old telegraph operator at the St. Paul and Duluth depot, wouldn't leave his post. He was concerned about the many passengers who had gathered at the depot to wait for the Limited and wanted to warn Engineer Jim Root of the trouble he would run into as he neared Hinckley. But Tom Dunn never got his message to Root. As the depot burned around him, Dunn sent his last communication north to Barnum: "I have stayed too long."

By 3.30 p.m. only balls of fire illumined the black sky and gas explosions sounded above the cyclonic wind. Families fled in pandemonium. About a hundred people managed to reach the town's gravel pit. A spring filled the hole with water even in dry weather. The entire population of Hinckley probably could have been saved there. While many had huddled in the gravel pit, others had crowded aboard the train at the Eastern Minnesota depot. As it headed toward Sandstone, the train crossed the burning

Kettle River bridge just minutes before it collapsed. The train continued on the smoky course to Superior and Duluth.

People who had missed the Eastern Minnesota train and others who were running for safety sought refuge in a nearby swamp. Flames leapt through the dry grass and reached "Death Swamp", where 127 suffocated. Those who succeeded in staying ahead of the fire met Jim Root's train. He loaded them aboard, put his engine in reverse and backed away from Hinckley. Six miles north was a marshy spot named Skunk Lake. The train crew and all 300 passengers were saved in its foul smelling water.

In all two hundred and forty-eight citizens of Hinckley died in a disaster which attracted publicity across the country and abroad. On Sunday, September 2, a headline on the front page of *The New York Times* read: "TWO MINNESOTA TOWNS UTTERLY DESTROYED BY FIRE." The Sunday editions of the St. Paul, Minneapolis and Duluth papers reported: "INFERNO IN FORESTS" and "HINCKLEY IS IN ASHES" On September 4 *The Times* of London told of the "GREAT FOREST FIRES IN AMERICA." Five days after the fire, Nellie Bly, the globet trotting journalist from the *New York World*, walked over the remnants of the burned villages and telegraphed a 5,000 word account to her editor. The entire country sent sympathy, money and supplies to the fire victims.

Vikingland, across the state from the Arrowhead area, has all the makings of a great vacation area. The Northwestern Minnesota region has ten state parks, some of the best duck hunting and walleye fishing in the state and a plethora of state wildlife management areas. However, the first stop for any visitor should be Itasca State Park for a cautious stepping across the stones or a leap over the gurgling headwaters of the Mississippi River before it begins its 2,500-mile journey to the Gulf of Mexico. It took three centuries for explorers to find the source of the Mississippi. Seven men claimed to have found it before Henry Rowe Schoolcraft proved them all wrong by finding the true head (Veritas caput), condensed to Itasca. Supposedly he and his Indians only spent two hours here in 1833, then turned around and went downstream to Fort Snelling before going all the way to New Orleans.

Two national wildlife refuges are located in Vikingland – Tamarac and Agassiz. Tamarac covers 42,725 acres of lakes, marshes and hillsides forested with both hardwoods and evergreens. Mallards, wood duck, deer, ruffed grouse, beaver, bald and golden eagles and herons populate the refuge. During annual migrations, nearly half a million ducks raft on the pools in Agassiz National Wildlife Refuge. Cormorants, peregrine falcons, a colony of Franklin gulls (25,000 pairs can sometimes be seen in the southeast corner of Agassiz Pool) and a herd of approximately 250 moose all lodge within the refuge. The moose are most easily seen along the roads in the early morning or at dusk.

Just south of Tamarac Refuge, in the middle of 412 lakes, is Detroit Lakes. To the west is Moorhead, twin city to Fargo, North Dakota. Moorhead's mustard-colored Solomon G. Comstock House was built in 1883 for the lawyer who wheeled and dealed with James J. Hill. Above Moorhead is the Red River Valley, an eighty-mile expanse of the state's most fertile farmland. It is the bed of the ancient, glacial Lake Agassiz. The flat land, saturated with rich black dirt, produces bountiful crops of malting barley, sugar beet and high-yield dwarf wheat.

Alexandria, which sits at the southern tip of Vikingland, bills itself as the "birthplace of America." Allegedly, Vikings visited Minnesota in 1360 and carved Norse symbols on the famed Kensington Runestone. "Big Ole," the world's largest Viking statue, stands guard near the Runestone Museum.

In between Vikingland and the Arrowhead area lies Minnesota's Heartland, and at its northern tip is the Northwest Angle. Everyone knows that, except for Alaska, the Northwest Angle of Minnesota is the nothernmost part of the United States. But few know how it got there. It was in truth the result of ignorance, accident and an astronomer's ruler. That Benjamin Franklin, John Adams and John Jay contributed to the confusion is understandable. It is more surprising that these fathers of our country knew anything about the remote Lake of the Woods.

The confusion began at the signing of the Treaty of Paris in 1783 at the conclusion of the American Revolutionary War, and did not end until the boundary was surveyed and explicitly established in 1925. In 1783, Franklin, Adams and Jay were among those representing the United States at the meeting to establish the treaty. After several proposals and counter proposals, the British ministry suggested that the boundary follow Rainy River "to the Lake of the Woods, thence through the said lake to the north western part thereof, and from thence on a due west course to the river Mississippi ..." There was a flaw in the proposition. The Mississippi is not west of the Lake of the Woods. In fact, it is 140 miles south. The negotiators had made the mistake of trusting "Mitchell's Map of North America," published in London in 1775.

The British were soon aware of the problem, and at the Treaty of Ghent they proposed that the negotiations be reopened. This time they asked that the line be defined from Lake Superior to the Mississippi. The government of the United States agreed that there was a problem, but was not willing to drop the border south of the Lake of the Woods to the Mississippi. If the United States had concurred with the British government, Canada would own the entire iron range.

A line had to be drawn and the surveyors couldn't cope with the irregular shoreline, the peninsulas and the bays. The United States boundary was in the hands of a British astronomer and his ruler. From the northernmost point of the Lake of the Woods he dropped a line straight south to the 49th parallel, thus creating the Northwest Angle of the United States. His decision was accepted by both sides.

The Heartland is the legendary stomping ground of Paul Bunyan and his sidekick, Babe the Blue Ox. Paul Bunyan was a French-Canadian lumberjack and, though he never stepped on American soil, Canadian loggers brought tales of him to their work in the United State's forests. By 1914, with the help of newspapers and magazines, all of America knew that Paul had gouged the Mississippi River to transport logs, and that his faithful Blue Ox had formed Minnesota's lakes with her great footprints. Heartland has 5,000 campsites, 1,000 resorts and 2,500 lakes which are filled with all sizes of fish from crappies to muskie. A great portion of those muskies are swimming in Walker's Leech Lake, and nearby Chippewa National Forest has the largest population of bald eagles in the world. Bemidji, claiming Paul Bunyan and Babe the Blue Ox as their very own, flaunts towering statues of them.

South of Bemidji, Brainerd, where tourism is the community's main industry, gets into the act with a Paul Bunyan Center. Brainerd was built and named by the Northern Pacific Railroad. During the late 1800s Brainerd, with 500 lakes surrounding the city, became a popular resort area. The best known are Breezy Point Resort on Big Pelican Lake and Gragun's Lodge, Grandview Lodge and Madden's, all on Gull Lake. Grandview is perhaps the most prestigious, but Madden's has the same amenities, and additional golf courses.

Going further south in the Heartland we find Little Falls, the boyhood home of American hero Charles A. Lindbergh. Nearby is Camp Ripley, the nation's largest National Guard training camp with more than 53,000 acres.

St. Cloud was founded in 1856. As the northernmost navigational point on the Mississippi River, it quickly became a significant Mississippi rivertown. Today, with a population of 42,500 it is Minnesota's fastest-growing community. St. Cloud is a college town, with St. Cloud State University in the city and the College of St. Benedict and St. John's University four miles north.

Just off the exit ramp at Collegeville, silhouetted against the sky, stands Marcel Breuer's monumental bell tower for St. John's Abbey and University. The disparity of the concrete banner arching over a countryside of silos, cattle and quarries, is jarring. The landmark leads the traveler to St. John's, the world's largest Benedictine abbey. It is also a highly respected liberal arts college for men.

The 300 monks who have made their vows to this abbey are monastic, but have a global perspective. They make it a point to visit parishes and missions and to continue their studies. On any given day one or other of the monks may be in the Colorado Rockies, in San Francisco, or in Ethiopia.

The Benedictine Order takes its name and instruction from Benedict of Nursia who lived from around 480 to 547. As abbot of the monastery at Monte Cassino, south of Rome, he wrote what he called "a little rule for beginners" that contained "nothing harsh, nothing burdensome." Benedict was a pious, tolerant man who advocated a balanced life and had a concern for the community. He wrote: "We read that monks should not drink wine at all, but since the monks of our day can't be convinced of this, let us at least agree to drink moderately, and not to the point of excess, for wine makes even wise men go astray." He also addressed the problem of reluctant early risers, "On arising for the Work of God, they will quietly encourage each other, for the sleepy like to make excuses." Benedict's counsel was wise. Above all, he stressed holiness and obedience to God.

In 1856, dispatched by Abbot Wimmer, five monks left Pennsylvania and made their way to St. Louis for the river trip north to St. Paul. Once in St. Paul they encountered a new problem, for their contact, Bishop Cretin, spoke only French and English and two of the monks spoke only German. The monks had been told that they were needed around Sauk Rapids. They headed in that direction and settled on temporary sites while battling a food shortage caused by locusts. Finally, in 1866, the monks found their permanent spot. They built the first of the buildings that would become part of the new monastery and soon Minnesota's second institution of higher learning was established.

In an isolated pocket below St. Cloud lie sand dunes. Sand Dunes State Forest is more representative of a desert then Minnesota's Heartland. However, there are no cacti or any other vegetation, just waves of sand.

West of St. Cloud lies Sauk Centre, a rather standard mid-American town. Had Sinclair Lewis not been born there it probably would have received no more fanfare than hundreds of other small market towns. As it turned out, Sinclair Lewis wrote a book about his native town, Sauk Centre, Minnesota, and became America's first Nobel Prize-winning author.

Main Street, Lewis' acerbic satire of "Gopher Prairie, Minnesota," was one of the most read and most denounced novels ever written by an American. The book first appeared in November 1920. Ten years later Lewis was awarded the Nobel Prize. Just twenty years later he died of a heart attack, on January 10, 1951, alone and disconsolate. Ironically, he died in Rome, the root of Western civilization; a Minnesota man who was never able to establish his own roots.

Harry Sinclair Lewis was born in Sauk Centre, Minnesota, on the frost-nipped morning of February 7, 1885. His mother, a fragile, timid woman, would die of tuberculosis before his seventh birthday. His father was Dr. E.J. Lewis, a country physician. Sauk Centre was a typical prairie hamlet – a marketplace for nearby grain and dairy farms. However, the formerly undistinguished town would be immortalized and Dr. Lewis' commonplace home would become a landmark.

Harry Lewis was an unpopular youngster. He was tall, gangly, homely (already suffering from a life-long skin disease) and inept at sports. Reading was both a pleasure and an escape. As a student at Yale, his isolation was exacerbated by his arrogance and verbosity. He became known on campus as "God-forbid." In time, his antidote to loneliness became alcohol. Lewis graduated from Yale in the summer of 1908 and returned to Sauk Centre. Three weeks later he was in Waterloo, Iowa, working on a newspaper. And from that time on he led the life of a vagabond.

For the next few years Lewis traveled to London, New York, and Paris, hobnobbing with exponents of the startling ideas of Marx, Darwin and Freud. In New York he spent time with the young intellectuals and artists of Greenwich Village who were bent on undermining America's traditional values. Though he shared their philosophy and was certainly most talented, he never did fit in with their subculture.

While Lewis moved around during the next few years, spending two of them in the Twin Cities, he wrote five novels. Then, in the autumn of 1920, he presented his major work. *Main Street* was an immediate sensation. Nearly every newspaper in the country, except the *Sauk Centre Herald*, commented on the caustic novel. Detractors, no less than enthusiasts, were buying and reading it.

However, Lewis' novels have not all passed the test of time. In the 1920s he was the undisputed champion of a group of literary heavyweights which included Hemingway, Fitzgerald and Dreiser. He was revered both in the U.S. and abroad. Today he is seldom read, but a visitor to Sauk Centre couldn't miss his relevance to that one Midwestern town. Main Street has been renamed The Original Main Street. The cross street, on which Dr. Lewis' home stands, is labeled Sinclair Lewis Avenue. Sauk Centre's only motion picture theater is the Main Street. The town's high school athletic teams are known as the Streeters. There is a Sinclair Lewis Park and Interpretive Center.

Throughout his early writing years Lewis was frequently in Minnesota, living for short periods in different places. He lived in a lemon-colored brick house on Summit Avenue in St. Paul and, later, moved to Mount Curve Avenue in Minneapolis. He slept in bunkhouses at Cass Lake lumber camps, visited friends on an island on Rainy Lake, and spent a summer in Mankato.

He returned to Minnesota in the 1940s, setting up residence in Duluth. Then he lived in Minneapolis while he taught a writing class at the University of Minnesota. Lewis was unimpressed with Minneapolis. He found "most buildings ... drab ... irregular in relationship to one another – a set of bad teeth." On the other hand he thought the Minnesota rural landscape very attractive and was particularly taken by the rocky, hilly farms and the tree-lined banks of the St. Croix Valley near Marine. In fact, Lewis was rapturous about the more photogenic sections of Minnesota. For posterity he listed the seven scenic areas which met with his approval. He began with the view of the St. Croix Valley as the traveler enters Taylors Falls from Highway No. 8. Second was the Leaf Mountains portion of Otter Tail County, with the sensational view of surrounding waters and woods from the top of Inspiration Peak. Third he noted most of Fillmore and Houston counties, chiefly the region adjacent to Chatfield, Lanesboro, and Preston. Next he mentioned the Mississippi River bluffs, stretching from Red Wing to La Crescent, a view which is reminiscent of New York's Hudson Valley. Finally he cited two lakes for their special appeal: Minnetonka and Minnewaska. As an afterthought he added the area around New London and Kandiyohi County. If Lewis had wandered north of Duluth he certainly would have given the North Shore of Minnesota a star for its remarkable beauty.

The region now called Minnesota was disputed by the Objibwa (corrupted to Chippewa) and the Sioux. Living too far north for substantial agriculture, the tribes were nomadic hunters, mainly dependent on the white-tailed deer, and buffalo. They also gathered maple syrup and wild rice. The Objibwa, pushed west by the white man, were forced to fight the Sioux for living space. The battle at the Objibwa camp at Crow Wing in 1768 was a definitive defeat for the Dakota, a tribe of the Sioux Nation.

Crow Wing was situated in the center of Minnesota, at the confluence of the Crow Wing and Mississippi rivers. The village, which burgeoned during the fur trading period, even survived the trade's decline. After a couple of decades, the Objibwa village and fur post at Crow Wing had developed into an outfitting center, serving ox-cart trains on the Woods-Red River Trail, which crossed the Mississippi at that point. By the 1860s the town had a population of 600, and more than thirty buildings. In the same decade, the battle between the Sioux and the Objibwa in Minnesota finally came to an end. However, the traditional enemies then succumbed to an even stronger foe – the white man.

The Sioux Uprising began in 1862 and lasted for sixteen

years. On August 18, Sioux Chief Little Crow led a surprise attack on settlers in the Minnesota Valley. Before the uprising was under control, as many as 800 white settlers and soldiers were killed, and acres of land were destroyed in Southern Minnesota. Measured in terms of lives lost, the outbreak was the worst in American history, and it launched a succession of Indian wars on the Northern Plains that did not end until 1890 with the battle of Wounded Knee in South Dakota.

During the same period that the Sioux were fighting for their rights, the Objibwa ceded their lands to the government and were concentrated into the Leech Lake Reservation. Today, nearly 5,000 Objibwa – Chippewa – live on that reservation. Wild rice is an important part of their economy, as it was for their ancestors. The palatable grain is abundant in several shallow lakes in Minnesota and Ontario. It sprouts in late April from seeds that settled into the mud the previous autumn. The submerged leaves bud in mid-May, the stem develops and the grass-like plant reaches the surface by early June. Once the wild rice grows a foot or two above the water, spikelets develop and carry the kernels which mature at different rates. The ripe grain detaches easily from the stem and takes several weeks to harvest. Unharvested rice falls to the bottom of the lake, starting the cycle once more.

The month of August was known as the rice moon, for it was the time of harvesting. It took two people to take in the harvest, often a man and his wife. The man poled a canoe gently through the tall grass of the rice stand and the woman held a short stick in each hand. With one stick she bent the stalks and with the other she thwacked the ripe kernels into the canoe. When the canoe was full, the couple went ashore and arranged the rice on birchbark mats where it dried. Then it was parched in an iron kettle to loosen the husks. To remove the husks, an Indian trod on the kernels in a shallow hole lined with deerskin. To steady himself, he held two poles tied to a sapling. Finally the wind carried off the chaff as the grain was repeatedly poured into birchbark winnowing trays. The refined rice was stored in woven birchbark bags sewn closed with basswood cord.

Wild rice, a fairly rare commodity, is considered a delicacy by many. Until the 1970s prices fluctuated widely, often becoming very high. The harvest was affected by too little or too much water and by the discrepancy in maturation. As a result, plant geneticists developed a domesticated form that could be grown in paddies By the mid-1970s Minnesota, the country's largest supplier of wild rice, had 17,000 acres of paddy rice, much of it north of the town of Aitkin. Paddy rice has its detractors, who claim that it is less tasty and grown using pesticides, but its existence has stabilized the supply, thereby lowering prices.

Stillwater joins Minneapolis and St. Paul in Metroland. Historical markers on its Main Street, at the north and south ends of the city, welcome visitors to "The Birthplace of Minnesota." That is misleading: Stillwater dates to 1843 and there were settlers at Grand Portage in the 1790s. Upstream from Stillwater, at Marine on the St. Croix, Minnesota's first sawmill was built in 1839. Southeast at Mendota, across from Fort Snelling, settlement had occurred even earlier. In 1835 twenty-four-year-old fur trader Henry Sibley built his two-story stone house on the Mississippi River site. This partner in the American Fur Company used his residence for business and, later, as Minnesota's first governor's mansion. A Fort Snelling census taken two years later listed seventy-five persons in Mendota.

Nevertheless, the Stillwater claim isn't too far afield. Until 1837 most of the present state of Minnesota was Indian territory. Only two fairly small pieces of land had actually been purchased from the Sioux. One of these was the site of Fort Snelling; the other was located at the mouth of the St. Croix. Lieutenant Zebulon Pike, on his way to find the headwaters of the Mississippi, had arranged this transference of land in 1895. He had not intended to defraud the Indians, yet that is exactly what he did.

The treaty signing with the Sioux leaders took place with much decorum under a shelter made from Pike's sails. The lands were at the confluence of the Minnesota and Mississippi rivers, south and west of the St. Croix. The land ceded totaled 100,000 acres, and Pike estimated the property as worth 200,000 dollars, but bequeathed the detail of payments to the government in Washington. In the meantime, he distributed 200 dollars in gifts and sixty gallons of liquor. More than a dozen years passed before Congress paid the Indians a parsimonious sum of 2,000 dollars.

In 1845, Nathaniel Fish Moore, the prestigious president of New York City's Columbia College, stopping at Stillwater en route to the Falls of St. Anthony, reported that the village had "a saw mill, a tavern, a country merchant's store, and some half dozen wooden houses." Three years later, there were five stores, two hotels, "a flourishing school," and about twenty-five "very neat and well-finished buildings." It is appropriate that Moore listed the sawmill first because without it the community wouldn't have existed. The same year in which Mr. Moore visited Stillwater, the town's first post office operated out of a corner in a general store.

Stillwater came of age in the years after the Civil War. Railroads were following the frontier and Stillwater lumbermen, who once sold their product exclusively downriver, were shipping lumber by rail as far west as Colorado. Two thousand men with 500 teams of horses harvested the forests in 1871 and came up with more than 145,000 feet of logs. The figure peaked in 1890 when a record 450,000 board feet of lumber came through the St. Croix Boom. Stillwater's population reached 18,000 and more than a few business barons made their fortunes.

At one time, four railroads ran through Stillwater, stopping at the Union Depot which was built in 1887 of brownstone quarried from the Apostle Islands. And two years later Stillwater's citizens rode Minnesota's first electric street cars (while in Minneapolis and St. Paul people were still being transported by horse cars).

Way back in the early 1850s, when the territorial legislature was choosing a capital for Minnesota, Stillwater was in the running. St. Paul was chosen, but Stillwater was awarded 20,000 dollars to build the state penitentiary; a necessity in a new territory. The three-story prison house with two "dungeons" was built in Battle Hollow (the site of the bloody confrontation between the Sioux and the Objibwa fourteen years).

Prison inmates were issued with hickory-dyed cloth shirts and gray pants, and with red and blue jackets and blanket-wool caps. One half of each prisoner's head was shaved. When numerous prisoners escaped with ease, "penitentiary stripes" were introduced to make the escapees more identifiable. The inmates now wore hip jackets, trousers and skull caps of heavy blanket cloth with alternating stripes. That was the regulation uniform until 1981.

Another Stillwater institution, the Lowell Inn, also attracted outsiders, but for much shorter stays. It is a favorite haunt for Twin Citians who enjoy the scenic drive, an elegant dinner in one of the Inn's cosmopolitan dining rooms and an overnight stay in a romantic, antique-laden bedroom.

The population of Stillwater diminished by more than half when the sawmill became obsolete in the late 1920s. Few had anticipated the inevitable, but the supply of select timber was not inexhaustible. It had taken lumbermen little more than fifty years to scour Minnesota's centuries-old pine forests. The "old-timers" looked on as the last log floated through the St. Croix Boom in 1914. Stillwater needed a new focus. Nelle and Arthur Palmer did their part to give the town a lift when they left vaudeville to run the Lowell Inn in 1930. But the place didn't catch on, mostly because Twin Citians couldn't find it. Palmer had an answer. He painted the telephone poles blue and white along the rural roads from Minneapolis to Stillwater, then placed advertisements in newspapers telling his potential customers to follow the novel guideposts to the inn. The poles didn't remain painted for long, but the Lowell Inn has since become a local landmark.

Back in the mid-1800s it would have taken more than half a day to travel the twenty miles from Stillwater to St. Paul. The means of transportation would have been stagecoach.

When all the territory west of the Mississippi was claimed by the United States, a number of Yankees journeyed to the far western reaches of the New World. Most of these frontiersmen who arrived in Minnesota in the 1800s neither regarded land as something to revere, as did the Indians, nor as something to conquer, as did the early explorers who were looking for gold. They weren't fleeing governmental or religious oppression, and they weren't searching for souls to win. Minnesota's settlers came to affirm their individualism. They wanted to make something of themselves and were willing to work hard to accomplish that goal. They were hardy souls – hardy enough to contend with inclement weather, loneliness and a more primitive lifestyle. There was wealth to be found in the fledgling territory of Minnesota – in lumber, iron ore, and fertile soil. And those who stuck with it did make something of themselves. Many even made it big.

One day Frederick Weyerhaeuser was left alone at a sawmill in Rock Island, Illinois. Soon a few farmers showed up wanting a load of lumber, which Weyerhaeuser sold to them. When his boss returned Weyerhaeuser handed him the sixty dollars in gold. "I was greatly relieved when Mr. Marsh approved of my performance," he said. "It was my first sale of lumber."

The lumber salesman's story began in Niedersaulheim, Germany, where he was born on November 21, 1834. His family was one of the wealthier in the small Rhine Valley town and owned a fifteen-acre farm and three-acre vineyard. Because times were hard in Germany, even for the financially stable, Weyerhaeuser's relatives were lured to the "good life" in America. At the age of twenty-three

he followed his family to the new land, settled in Pennsylvania and became a brewer. Four years later he headed for Rock Island because of its "richness of soil", and was eventually employed by the Rock Island Lumber Co.

Shortly after his historic first sale of lumber he met Sarah Elizabeth Bloedel, who came to visit her older sister, Anna Catherine Denkmann, in Rock Island. Weyerhaeuser and Miss Bloedel, who also came from Niedersaulheim, were married in Denkmann's house about seven months later.

In 1860 Weyerhaeuser and his brother-in-law Frederick Carl August Denkmann pooled their resources and bought a bankrupt lumber mill. Their lumber business burgeoned, even though it was necessary to trade for farmer's hogs, horses, oxen and eggs. These they exchanged for supplies from merchants and made a good profit. "To my great astonishment ..." said Weyerhaeuser, "we made 3,000 dollars in the first nine months and 5,000 dollars in the second year. Eventually, he and Denkmann owned the Rock Island Lumber Manufacturing Co. and four other lumber-related businesses. Weyerhaeuser had interests in eighteen additional companies. He once told a friend who questioned whether a potential purchase would result in a profit "whenever I buy timber I make a profit. When I do not buy I miss an opportunity." Another time he told reporters that his success was the result of "paying more attention to his credit than his clothes."

Weyerhaeuser's greatest strength, however, was his ability to recognize competent men and bring them together. As his businesses expanded, he waded into new adventures and invited his partners to join him. When his partners were reluctant he asked, "Is it all right if I do it all on my own?" That seemed to be the right incentive. Perhaps out of fear of missing an opportunity, the partners bought into the new deal and became wealthy in spite of themselves.

Weyerhaeuser was a quiet, self-effacing man. All of his life he was conscious of the German accent he brought to America as a young man. When a woman approached him at a social gathering and asked, "Mr. Weyerhaeuser, why don't you take part in the conversation?" he reportedly answered, "I have two eyes to see with, two ears to hear with, but I only have one mouth and I use it to eat "

Weyerhaeuser was a family man. He wrote chatty letters to his "dearest Sarah" when he went into the "pineries," and she was proud of "her Fritz." He gave each of his grandchildren copies of "Poor Richard's Almanac" underlining such sentences as "God helps those who help themselves."

The lumber industry was fully developed in the 1880s and, as timber fell like dominoes, the lumbermen moved west. At the same time as the lumber business reached its maturity, Weyerhaeuser reached his fifties and was a multi-millionaire. Adding to his numerous enterprises, he had formed the Mississippi River Logging Company with sawmill men including P.M. Musser and Thomas Irvine, whose descendents still live in St. Paul and remain stockholders in the Weyerhaeuser Company.

In 1891 Weyerhaeuser moved his family to St. Paul and bought a home at 266 Summit Avenue. His choice of residence was not influenced by the fact that his next door neighbor was railroad magnate James J. Hill. The two men had antithetic personalities. Hill liked the limelight every bit as much as Weyerhaeuser liked to be behind the scenes. Still, their ambitions were similar. With pioneers' spirit, each man pushed west to build his empire, and fourth generation descendents linked the barons of business when Weyerhaeuser's great grandson, John Driscoll, married Hill's great granddaughter, Elizabeth Slade.

James Hill was born in Ontario, Canada, in 1838. His brother, Alec, was less than a year younger and a close companion. One day, eight-year-old Alec asked Jim to make him a bow and arrow. Jim was an excellent shot with the rifle and a skilled fisherman. Influenced by passages in the Bible, he decided to expand his sports equipment and made bows and arrows from the materials he found in his untamed environment. But on this day the bow snapped and the end of the arrow which was held, under tension, close to his right eye was propelled backward and the eye was badly injured. The next year James Jerome Hill's father died and his formal education ended. For four years he worked at several jobs in Canada and then decided that the world held something better for him.

So James J. Hill left home and headed for the eastern United States, where he would spend some time before embarking on his journey to the Orient. His baggage was light but he wore a tall, felt "Horace Greely hat" to cover up his youthful appearance. The hat was slightly large but it was the best he could find. Thus attired, he climbed aboard the Grand Trunk Railway express to Toronto. As the train lurched forward, the hat tumbled off his head and disappeared into the distance. But it didn't matter, Hill was on his way and besides, where he was going the climate would be warmer.

Hill's odyssey in America is best described in a letter to his grandmother:

"It is with a feeling of greatest pleasure that I undertake to keep my word with you by writing as soon as I was settled. After I left Canada I went direct to New York and there I had a slight mishap which caused no injury except a pecuniary one. After leaving New York I went to Philadelphia, Baltimore, Charleston, Savannah and Pittsburgh, spending a good deal of time and money, and afterwards I came back to New York. I took a notion to go and see St. Paul. I like this country very well and I think I shall like it better the longer I live here. I am in the commission and shipping business. My salary is twice as much as I could get in Canada and work is easy, all done in an office. I have from 6 o' clock every evening to walk around and enjoy myself."

The "notion to go and see St. Paul" had been brewing in Hill's mind for a long time. He had the pioneer spirit that nudged him to the edge of the frontier or, at least, to a jumping-off point like St. Paul. The works of Henry Clay Daniel Webster, Stephen A. Douglas and Dred Scott played an important role in the politics of the 1850s. The ultimate result of various acts and decisions was the reinforcement of the attractiveness of the upper Midwest. The year after Hill arrived in St. Paul, Harriet Bishop summarized a few of the unique aspects of the new city: "St. Paul is comparatively an infant city, with a population of probably 10,000 souls, but here 'every man counts.' Here, men are picked not from the fossilized haunts of old fogyism, but from the swiftest blood of the nation. Every man here, to use a western expression, 'is a steamboat,' and is determined to make his mark on the history of Minnesota... It is a strange medley indeed, that which you meet aboard a Mississippi steamer. An Australian gold hunter, a professor in an eastern university going out to invest in Minnesota, a South Carolina boy, with 1,000 and a knowledge of double-entry bookkeeping ..."

Although Bishop may have oversold the rough frontier village of St. Paul, there is no doubt that its position on the Mississippi River promoted it as a transportation center for the Midwest. The tremendous opportunities in the new railroad industry weren't fully realized in 1855 and the steel industry boom was yet to come. Two years earlier the railroad had connected Chicago with the river, but it would be eleven years before railtrack would link St. Paul, to Chicago. Meanwhile, the steamboat was in its heyday and, within hours of his arrival in St. Paul, young Hill was investigating steam boating on the Mississippi. Soon Hill was in the river-transportation business, making a strong impression on all his older associates. He was a willing and able worker and had good business sense.

St. Paul was still importing flour when Hill arrived, but would soon become the greatest flour milling center in the United States. Above St. Paul, the Falls of St. Anthony supplied unlimited water power. There the first commercial grist mill was erected. But a new problem emerged. The mills ground right through the winter while ice formed on the river. So warehousing of the temporary surplus became necessary until railroads came to the rescue. The St. Paul and Pacific Railroad began to haul flour and other goods in from St. Anthony Falls in 1862. Hill was there to help load the wooden freight cars, but he would prove his business prowess in various fields, including wholesale merchandising with Temple and Beaupré and later with Borup and Champlin, before specializing in railroads.

In 1867 Hill signed an agreement with the St. Paul and Pacific which would give him control of the railroad's entire riverside terminal facilities in St. Paul. The St. Paul and Pacific was vital to transportation between Duluth and the Pacific Ocean, but when the Northern Pacific gained control of the line in 1870, its significance was limited to Minnesota alone. The powerful Northern Pacific was financed by Jay Cooke, who also financed the Civil War for the Federal Government. Before long, the farsighted Hill voiced his strong opinions. During his twenty years in St. Paul he had come to be regarded as the best expert on railroad economics in the Midwest, and he developed much further-reaching plans for the St. Paul and Pacific. He saw it as a carrier of traffic between the Twin Cities and Winnipeg through the Red River Valley, and within the United States between Saulte Ste. Marie on the East and St. Vincent on the West.

Hill's vision for railroads continued to be larger than life. He bought into and headed up many lines, which culminated in his role as chairman of the board of the Great Northern Railroad. In 1912 he drafted a twenty-three page letter of resignation in the form of a farewell to his fellow workers: "... most men who have really lived have had, in some shape, their great adventure. This railway is mine. I feel that a labor and a service so called into being, touching at so many points the lives of so many millions with its ability to serve the country, and firmly established credit and reputation, will be the best evidence of its permanent value and that it no longer depends upon the life or labor of any single individual."

Minnesota came to be known as the "Gopher State" as a direct result of a cartoonist's portrayal of some people's disenchantment with the railroad promoters. He drew the railroad men as striped gophers to equate them with the pesty gophers that destroyed crops.

In 1855 John Sargent Pillsbury made a decision that would reverberate through four generations. He resisted the lure of California's gold and settled near St. Anthony, Minnesota, where the combination of timber, water power and river transportation suggested a site for a potential business.

He established a hardware store which was first threatened by the panic of 1857 and then succumbed to a fire that wiped out its 40,000 dollar inventory. Pillsbury and his wife lived like paupers for the next six years as he paid his creditors in instalments, often as small as twenty-five dollars. His integrity was noted. When the Farmers and Mechanics Bank made the first loan of its 8,000 dollars in deposits, it was to John Pillsbury: 1,000 dollars at twelve percent. A little while later he was offered the presidency of F. and M. He declined.

After a few years he persuaded his nephew, Charles Alfred, to leave New Hampshire and join him in Minneapolis. So Charles and his bride, Mary Ann Stinson, headed west.

In 1869 John, Charles and George Pillsbury gathered together 10,000 dollars for their one-third partnership in a dilapidated Minneapolis flour mill. Charles would manage the mill, located on the southeast corner of First Street and Sixth Avenue South. To compensate for his services, he would receive 1,000 dollars a year plus one-sixth of the net earnings. The percentage of earnings proved an effective incentive for Charles. By the end of the year his portion of the profit was 6,000 dollars. Two years later he formed his own firm, C.A. Pillsbury and Company.

But the Pillsburys were never satisfied with just making a living. They came from a lineage of high achievers and community-minded citizens. John S. got into politics, first as state senator and then for three terms as governor. Historians tell us that he missed his own inauguration. On the big day, in 1875, he was traveling incognito, by wagon, trying to assess the extent of the grasshopper affliction in the state.

He also established the University of Minnesota in a building which had as tenants a caretaker, his turkeys and an inadequate cow. Then the governor recruited the university's first student, a reluctant Easterner, and the school was offically launched.

Like the Pillsburys who came after him, John S. maintained a low profile – even as governor. An admirer wrote, in 1898 "... were it not for the public press, a person might live next door to Governor Pillsbury for a decade without learning what he had accomplished." George A., the governor's brother, chose an equally energetic course. He sat on many community boards and was elected an alderman of Minneapolis and, later, its mayor.

Meanwhile, the company continued to expand along with the region. In 1890, Charles A. made a hard-headed business decision. He sold the company to British investors, who took all the common stock and paid the family with preferred stock. Charles stayed on to oversee the company. He drew the largest salary of any American executive until, at fifty-seven years of age, he went to Egypt, hoping that the climate would ameliorate his poor health. Within eleven years, John, George and Charles Pillsbury were dead and the company was bankrupt.

But Charles Alfred's two boys, John and Charles, decided to do something to help. Immediately after graduating from college, they took their inherited preferred stock and made a deal with the British to lease the property from the bankrupt company. Eventually they bought it all back. Not until 1923, however, was the Pillsbury Company wholly owned by Americans again.

They called it "Washburn's Folly." For, as everyone in the frontier village of Minneapolis knew, a stone mill of six stories, costing an exorbitant 100,000 dollars (including equipment transported all the way from Buffalo) could not possibly make it. The mill would produce more flour than existing markets could handle.

But Cadwallader Washburn ignored the scoffers. In 1866 he completed his mill, later called the "B mill." A short time later Washburn left the Minneapolis Mill Company in his brother's hands while he offered his services in the Civil War. Despite his brother's mercurial, approach to business, and the threat of the St. Anthony Falls drying up, the mill survived. When Cadwallader returned, he transformed "a trade into a science" by developing techniques to produce a superior product.

Finally the two men who would have the most influence on Washburn's milling enterprises joined him. They would survive Washburn and carry on his work. John Crosby came from Bangor, Maine. He was a strong, stocky, well-liked man, popularly known as "Honest John." William Hood Dunwoody had an aristocratic appearance, a gentle manner and was a Quaker from Philadelphia. Together they helped Washburn develop what would become Wash burn Crosby, but it was the Bell family that would have the most enduring association with the milling company. James Stroud Bell made his debut in milling with Washburn Crosby in 1888 and, in 1928, James Ford Bell orchestrated the formation of General Mills. He and John Crosby II set out to develop new plants, new fields, new projects, new products, new responsibilities and to acquire new men. Bell declared: "There is no limit to the possibilities before us. The door is wide open."

He was right. General Mills' stock kept rising, even through the early 1930s when most of American industry was in distress. The progress can be attributed in part to Bell's insistence on a program of diversification. However, not all of General Mills' successful undertakings were planned. One of its most famous products came about completely by accident.

A hospital clinician preparing a bran gruel for patients spattered a few drops on the hot stove. The drops of gruel formed thin, round wafers. He made more of the crisp, tasty morsels. After demonstrating his discovery at General Mills, the clinician was supplied with mixing bowls and a hot plate. Soon a sample of the first batch was sealed and preserved as a master model. The commercial product matched it in quality, and the ready-to-eat cereal was available to market in November 1924. All it needed was a name. A contest was held among employees and their families, and Jane Bausman, in New York, suggested "Wheaties." She knew America's propensity for nicknames. Before long, a new song asked a simple question of the public:

"Have you tr-r-ried Wheaties?
They're whole wheat with all of the bran.
Won't you tr-r-r-y Wheaties?
For wheat is the best food of man."

The public responded positively and Wheaties soon became the "Breakfast of Champions."

General Mills next merchandising tour de force was the creation of Betty Crocker. She would have a certain set of values and she would become the quintessence of a housewife – all-wise and generous with time, advice and sympathy. Above all, she would be trustworthy. Another company contest was held to find the most Betty Crocker-like hands. Finally, she would have a carefully defined physical appearance, with Scandinavian, Irish and other European features meant to represent an all-American look. No one could have predicted the value of Betty Crocker's composed, reassuring sensible image to General Mills. But time proved the worth of America's first lady of food.

"Think it big and keep it simple" was one of J.F. Bell's characteristically succinct statements. General Mills did get big with Cheerios, vitamins and Bisquick. Cheerios were made from cooked dough which was pressed through a die and then expanded in a puffing gun. A well-muscled man was depicted in cartoon advertisements, performing such superhuman feats as juggling anvils. The accompanying caption read: "He's feeling his Cheerioats." Three years after its debut, Cheerioats became Cheerios. The word "oats" being claimed to deserve universal ownership; too generic to be incorporated in a specific product's name.

General Mills used one of the most successful radio serials, "The Lone Ranger," to further promote Cheerios. And, at one time, General Mills claimed to be the world's largest distributors of airplanes – the kind that come in boxes in the form of premiums. Package designers, scientists, laboratory technicians, experts in market analysis, conductors of surveys, psychologists and radio entertainers all had a part in carrying Cheerios to market.

The research laboratories were engaged in developing cereal products for manufacture in the home plant, as well as collaborating with other laboratories, like those of Eastman, in the development and distribution of new goods. General Mills followed another of Bell's dictums – diversification. Eventually the company became involved in games, toys, clothes and other commodities while keeping its focus on food.

William Wallace Cargill was born in 1844 on the East Coast. During his teenage years he worked on the Wisconsin farm of his father, a retired Scottish sea captain. When the Civil War ended and the frontier enlarged once again, Will Cargill set out on his own. He made enough money stacking grain in a flathouse along the railroad tracks in Conover, Iowa, to purchase five elevators in Austin, Minnesota, where he moved with his bride and two brothers in 1868. Those small wooden buildings were only a start.

Before Will Cargill died in 1909, he and his younger brothers, Sam, Jim and Sylvester had built or bought grain elevators and warehouses in more than 100 locations in Minnesota, North and South Dakota, Iowa and Wisconsin. Cargill created a "moving belt" of grain that transported wheat from countryside depots all the way to Chicago, and he hauled coal back through the same small towns. The company's success was assured, or so it seemed. However, the years that followed Will's death were shaky for Cargill, mostly because of the equivocal business ventures outside the grain industry made by Will's oldest son, William S. Cargill.

The company's champion was Will Cargill's son-in-law, John H. MacMillan. The son of Duncan D. MacMillan, a wealthy La Crosse businessman, John MacMillan was the same age as William S. Cargill. He brought his strict upbringing and his business experience – he was only fifteen when he went to work at his father's bank – to the Cargill Company. He battled to put the company back on its feet and, by 1917, had paid off the debts and completely reorganized the company, including buying out the twenty-five percent owned by William S. Cargill.

Today, Cargill is the largest grain-trading company in the world, with thirty-five branch offices in such places as Switzerland, Guatemala and Thailand. Cargill markets and processes dozens of commodities, including cotton, molasses, metals and poultry and, unlike other companies of its size, it is in the firm control of family members.

The Daytons, founders of Dayton-Hudson, are considered by many to be the most generous of the region's philanthropists. In 1978 Dayton-Hudson gave away nearly eight million dollars of its pre-tax profits for community use. The Daytons, in fact, began the Minneapolis Five Percent Club, an organization of businesses that annually turn over five percent of their pre-tax income – the maximum federal government allows companies to deduct from their taxes – for civic causes.

Daytons' was founded in the early 1900s by George Draper Dayton. Today's oldest generation, a group of five brothers, has gradually moved away from the family firm and into other ventures. Wallace, the third oldest, abandoned his job as president of Dayton Development Co. in 1968 "to get into something more meaningful."

He is now involved with six wildlife and land conservation groups, including the Nature Conservancy, for which he was once state chairman. Donald is regarded as "father" of Nicollet Mall, Minneapolis's magnificent main street. Bruce is scion of the arts. Kenneth marshalled construction of Orchestra Hall, and Douglas led the YMCA renaissance.

From the air, the Twin Cities appear as one: a lake-dotted, tree-lined metropolis with only the blue Mississippi River coiling between them. Home for over two million Minnesotans, half the state's population, the two cities reign jointly as the commercial and cultural capital of the upper Midwest. Each downtown area soars above the riverbanks. Minneapolis with blocks of tall glass and concrete buildings, and St. Paul with its historical architecture interspersed among the glass and concrete.

St. Paul's respect for the past is evidenced in its many renovated buildings, while Minneapolis proffers innovation, competition and progress – it's more a big city. St. Paul is heavily Roman Catholic, with ethnic parishes and a large Irish population. It is a government town, submerged in politics; the State Capitol dome competes with St. Paul's Cathedral to crown the skyline. In Minneapolis the fifty-seven-story Investors Diversified Services (IDS) Tower is the tallest building between Chicago and the Pacific.

The hundreds of parks and dozens of lakes within the cities and their suburbs make a beautiful setting. That beauty, combined with some more unequivocal indicators, including housing, income, education, government, health care, environment and recreation, caused the Urban Institute of Washington D.C. to rank the Twin Cities number one for overall quality of life.

Why? Some suggest that many of the area's founding fathers came from northern Europe, bringing an emphasis on good government with them. Others note that the inclement weather creates hardy citizens who unite against their common foe. Serious minority or crime problems are infrequent. Population density is low, single-family homes predominate, and going to church is still important. Also, the Twin Cities are surrounded by farm land, where old-fashioned values and the love of land are dominant. The cosmopolitan aspect of the big cities blends nicely with the Twin Cities' appreciation of the great outdoors.

Minnesota means "sky-tinted waters" in the language of the Dakota, and those waters molded its character. The Twin Cities' two most illustrious lakes are at the extremes of the city limits. White Bear, twelve miles northeast of St. Paul, and Minnetonka, fouteen miles west of Minneapolis, are popular playgrounds for sports enthusiasts. Five million people around the world do it. It's not quite sailing and it's not quite surfing but, from its beginning in the 1960s, boardsailing (also known as windsurfing) has become one of the world's major new sports. Windsurfing was even included in the 1984 Olympic Games in Los Angeles. People aged eight to eighty can windsurf anywhere they can find enough water to glide over and enough wind to keep them moving. The sport doesn't favor muscles. In fact, women sometimes pick it up faster than men because they don't try to power the board. What you have is a surf board about ten feet long and a sail which can rotate 360°C degrees. There are no ropes, just a mast and a boom. The windsurfer stands on the board and pulls the boom in to capture the wind, and releases it to let the wind spill out. As for many sports, the requisites are concentration and balance.

There is world-wide windsurfing competition. Some people have traveled to Guam to participate. But Lake Minnetonka windsurfers can stay at home and regional partakers in the sport don't have far to go to compete. The first Minnetonka Crossing was held in 1981. Seventy-five racers sailed 5.2 miles between the lakeside villages of Excelsior and Minnetonka. In 1984, 170 racers came from as far as Chicago to participate in the Minnetonka Crossing.

Another Minnesota sport which is generally uncelebrated is ice boating. This sport has been around a long time. Though it is appreciated only by the adventurous, its popularity would be extended if it weren't totally dependent on weather. To ice boat, the water must be frozen to at least a relatively safe depth and be free of snow. This rules out winters with early snow storms and fast spring thaws. However, there are usually a couple of days at the beginning and end of the winter season for the courageous sailors to have some fun. They put a plank over the open water between shore and ice and climb out to their boats.

An ice boat is six to thirty feet long, has a one- or two-man cockpit, blades on either side, and sails designed to speed the craft three times faster than the wind. Speeds of ninety miles per hour can be reached. The ride is cold, fast and bumpy. A helmet, goggles, face mask and down jacket are essential gear. As the sailor jibes and tacks he keeps an eye on the ice. He looks for black ice and tries to avoid heaves and cracks because there is the ever present danger of taking a nose dive into open water. If a boat does become stuck prow-first in an ice crack, its sailor will have to slide down it, over the prow and squat on the ice, crawling to spread his weight, on his hands and feet. If he goes through the ice he has to dog paddle to thicker ice. But an ice boat sailor wears a lot of clothing which becomes heavy when water-soaked, inhibiting his mobility. Just ten minutes in the icy water can be fatal.

Russell Bennett, who lives in Deephaven, Minnesota, a village on lake Minnetonka, knows all about the dangers of ice boating and the chill of winter's water. In 1958, he, David Wyer and Douglas Peterson sailed into a dreaded pressure ridge. Wyer's boat went through it and he clung to the hull. Bennett stopped his boat and ran toward Wyer, but the surface broke under him, dropping him into the lake. Clutching a broken chunk of ice, he trod water. Nearby hockey players threw him their sticks, Peterson tried to reach him with the mast of his boat, and a young boy was unable to crawl to him without beginning to go through. Bennett had been in the water twenty minutes when Tom Leaf, a ten-year-old weighing sixty-seven pounds, was instructed by police to use a rope and a board to rescue Bennett. Bennett was twenty-nine years old and weighed 225 pounds. His soaked clothing brought his weight to 350 pounds. The ice kept breaking as the policemen tried to pull him onto firm ice and he was eventually pulled out about forty yards from where he had first gone through. It took another fifteen minutes to get him to shore where he was given oxygen by a neighborhood doctor. Bennett finally arrived at a hospital where physicians agreed that only someone in his fine physical condition could have lived through the ordeal.

Another ice boating incident for Russell Bennett did not have life and death implications but it did have potential international consequences. Lord Mountbatten, a British naval commander, statesman and grandson of Queen Victoria, was visiting Minneapolis' General Mills in the 1960s. Lord Mountbatten wanted to go ice boating and Russell was asked to provide his boat. So he got his boat ready and soon Lord Mountbatten arrived at Lake Minnetonka dressed in a business suit with a white silk scarf tied around his neck. Russell gave him some warm clothing, and Mountbatten sailed over the icy lake with his long white scarf trailing behind him. His three aides and Bennett held their breath as they watched him jibe and tack at high speeds. Before long he was safely back on shore, glowing with another triumph to add to the lengthy list he had compiled over the years

Most of Minnesota's waters are used for more conventional sports. The state licenses about a million and a half fishermen each year and about 400,000 boaters and canoeists. The majority of anglers fish for fun but commercial fishermen still make a living out of the water of Lake of the Woods and Lake Superior. Fortunately, the sea lamprey which nearly wiped out Lake Superior's trout population in the 1920s have been effectively controled with chemicals in recent years.

Between 1835 and 1841 the American Fur Company sponsored the first commercial fishing operations on Lake Superior at Grand Portage and Isle Royal. Fish were plentiful but marketing was a problem. Following the copper "rush" in 1856 and 1857, settlers moved in around Lake Superior, hoping to earn an income from fishing. But it wasn't until the 1870s that the Lake Superior and Mississippi and the Northern Pacific railroads provided a means to market the fish.

The cisco (or chub) was the major commercial fish from the late 1800s up to the 1920s. At one point during the 1930s Lake Superior supplied about seventy-eight percent of the country's herring. In 1946 salt-water smelt first appeared in Lake Superior and are currently the dominant commercial fish. In 1951, 6,000 pounds of the silver-colored fish were harvested. The harvest has increased ever since, with a record catch of 2.9 million pounds of them in 1976. "Smelting" has become a spring tradition for many sports fishermen who are found with their nets dipped in tributary streams from Duluth to Grand Portage. Crowds gather around campfires or at the waters' edge with beer in hand to await the nocturnal run of smelt.

The railroads made it possible for fishermen to establish a remunerative business on Lake of the Woods. At the turn of the century the usual price for northern pike was three cents a pound and four cents for walleyes. And fish could be used for barter. In the 1890s seven sturgeon (the smallest of which was forty pounds) were traded for one cotton shirt. Before the turn of the century, sturgeon made up over one half of the continent's commercial catch and Lake of the Woods was one of the principal sources of this giant remnant of the glacial age – a 238 pounder set the record.

Eventually sturgeon became nearly extinct and whitefish all but so. In 1941 the Minnesota Legislature set size limits for sauger, walleye, northern pike and whitefish. Catching muskellunge, bass and crappies for pay was made illegal. This decision has been reversed in part. Today, however, most commercial fishing on Lake of the Woods is a family affair.

Recreational fishing in Minnesota does not dwindle for any appreciable amount of time. From mid-May through September, and then again for winter fishing under the ice, fishermen flock to the state's lakes. Lower Red Lake, with 180,868 acres of water and sixty-nine miles of shoreline, is the largest body of water entirely within Minnesota's borders. Upper Red Lake is the fourth largest, exceeded only by Mille Lacs Lake and Leech Lake.

Together, they represent the southern remnant of Lake Agassiz – the great inland sea that was formed by the melting of the Pleistocene Glacier. Once larger than the Great Lakes, its remains are still imposing. In addition to Red Lake it includes Lake of the Woods, Lake Winnipeg, Lake Manitoba and scores of smaller lakes.

On almost any Minnesota lake, fishermen are entertained by the haunting and magical sound of the loon – the state bird – and are annoyed by the irritating buzz of the mosquito, the unofficial state bird. Walleyes, panfish, northern and muskie can be found at Leech Lake and so can Camp Fish, the only fishing instruction camp in the world. Aspiring fishermen, aged seven to seventeen receive comprehensive training which covers making and maintaining equipment, fishing techniques, boat and water safety and fresh water biology and ecology. Moms and Dads are invited to special sessions. The camp sponsors programs which work in conjunction with Camp Courage, the affiliate of Courage Center, an institution which serves the handicapped.

Fish are caught in Minnesota streams too. Trout fishermen wade into the brushy, cold creeks of the Arrowhead country with fly rod in hand and cast for brook trout. The fisherman would know his favorite stream if he were blindfolded. Each has a distinctive smell. Whether it's sweet fern, jack pine, white cedar or reed canary grass, the scent is unmistakable.

The sounds along a river are unique too. Canoeists hear the roar of rapids or the swish of paddles in quiet moving water. The symphonic harmony of bird song, buzzing of insects, croaking of amphibians, the whistle of winds in the treetops and the splash of the giant leaping brown trout are all welcome sounds to the river wanderer. The night's first lonesome call of the whippoorwill signals the time to take fly rod in hand and head for the secret pool.

Wild flowers along stream banks and in marshy woods provide a kaleidoscope of color. Bloodroot is a harbinger of spring. A little later the marsh marigold, or cowslip, appears at the edge of stream banks, oxbow marshes and small tributary springs, sprinkling the lowlands with bright yellow. Soon, spring flowers appear in profusion – pink spring beauties, yellow bellworts, pristine white trilliums, purple and yellow violets, trout lilies with purple and green mottled leaves and Minnesota's state flower, the showy pink and white lady's slipper. Late in the summer or in early fall, gold jewelweed, or touch-me-not, line the water's rim, and brilliant red Indian paintbrush embellish gravel bars. Wild cherries, berries, grapes, plums and apples enhance the backpacker's journey and can be enjoyed on the trail, around a campfire, back at the cabin in front of the fire or much later, when the fruits are transformed into jams and jellies.

Minnesota's waters, split by a three-way continental divide within its borders, reach the Gulf of Mexico by way of the Mississippi River; the Atlantic Ocean through Lake Superior and the Great Lakes-St. Lawrence system, and turn toward the Arctic Ocean via the Red River of the North. Because Minnesota lies on the transitional point between eastern woodlands and western prairies, from the coniferous forest to the corn belt, and incorporates three drainage systems – the variety of streams is almost limitless. The moving waters creep through beaver meadows and wild rice flats, uncoil over high, tree-lined bluffs, and rush down mountainsides and through rocky gorges.

The rivers of Minnesota were the thoroughfares of Indians, explorers and trappers. Frontiersmen settled beside them, determining the present location of cities and towns. Minnesota's borders are outlined largely by its border streams – the Red River to the North, and the Rainy, Pigeon, St. Louis, St. Croix and Mississippi rivers. These rivers still serve as major navigational routes, but they also serve as playgrounds. Whether by snowshoe or cross-country ski, with rod and reel or shotgun in hand, the river valleys are used extensively by leisure seekers.

The center of Minnesota's canoe, fishing and hiking country is Ely, and Ely is the gateway into the Boundary Waters Canoe Area – the nation's only federally protected wilderness canoe area, which incorporates 1,200 miles of canoe routes and 2,000 designated campsites. The boundary waters can lead an adventurer to untouched territory.

B.R. Parks helped bring All American Championship Dog Sled Races to Ely. Straining against harnesses, the Alaskan malamutes, capable of pulling 100 pounds each, were exercised in Superior National Forest by Parks' son, John. Once vital for winter transport, dog teams gave way to the snowmobile, developed by Minnesotans. In recent years, every thirteenth resident has acquired one. Racers compete in an "International 500" on a course between Winnipeg, Manitoba, and St. Paul. Offering 39,000 dollars in prize money, the Minnesota capital sponsors the contest during its Winter Carnival.

Cross-country skiers complain that snowmobiles defile the silence and disturb the wildlife. They prefer to hear the whisper of skis passing over the snow and nature's sounds which can only be heard in near silence. Some favor the wilderness unalleviated by companionship. The lone skier or camper can hear the cry of the sleepy nuthatch, and other birds as they settle down for the night. Human voices mask nature's noises.

Undaunted by below-freezing temperatures downhill skiers in Minnesota swarm to the plethora of slopes. Lutsen, on the North Shore, is a particularly beautiful ski area and Buck Hill, in Burnsville – a suburb of Minneapolis – has hosted several national races with star performers like Pepi Gramshammer, André Molterer, Spider Savich and Jean Claude Killy. Olympic gold medalist Cindy Nelson trained at Buck Hill. Since 1891, Minnesota has had a championship team in curling, the sport where a forty-two-pound stone skids down a long, narrow strip of ice toward a six-foot target zone. The state has winners in another ice sport too. Eveleth has sent thirteen players to the National Hockey League; four of them are honored in Eveleth's United States Hockey Hall of Fame.

The Minnesota Boat Club was founded by keen rowers in 1870. Today the club enjoys the distinction of being the state's oldest institution. It has been located on St. Paul's Navy Island since 1873. A list of the club's membership over the years includes governors, mayors of St. Paul, and architect Cass Gilbert. Its fourth president was Governor William R. Merriam. Several Ellerbes, Griggs, Butlers, Weyerhaeuser's and Ordways have also been members.

Sailing is another vintage Minnesota sport. Boats are dotted over the waters of Lakes Waconia, Pepin, Superior, Mille Lacs, Forest Lake and the St. Croix River at Hastings.

The rivalry between Minneapolis and St. Paul was acted out in Minnesota's first sailing regatta in 1895, a contest which drew attention from as far away as Boston and New York. Lake Minnetonka's first fleet of sailboats appeared in 1882 and, in 1887, the Minnetonka Yacht Club was formed. Shortly thereafter the St. Paul Yacht Club began sailing on White Bear Lake.

It didn't take long for the two clubs to engage in serious debate concerning who had the better sailors. To settle the question, the St. Paul club proposed a series of regattas. In them, St. Paul sailed to become the undisputed champions in front of thousands of spectators from regional states, Massachusetts and New York. In recent years several Minnetonka Yacht Club superstars have raced their scows to national victories.

However, Minnesotans do participate inland sports too. Those who aren't on water could be on a golf course, tennis court, or inside playing racquet ball at the esteemed Commodore Hotel courts in St. Paul, or one of several other places. Or they could be horse riding on a polo field or through pastures, around a ring, over fences, or following fox hounds. However they do it, horseback riding is alive and well in Minnesota.

Minnesotans are proud of their professional teams too. They draw more spectators than the well-attended cultural events. Football's Minnesota Vikings, baseball's Minnesota Twins, hockey's North Stars and soccer's Strikers entertain hordes of Twin Cities' fans.

Minnesotans are immersed in another tradition that has nothing to do with water or lakes. Vice President Hubert J. Humphrey once quipped that, contrary to what one might think, there was no provision in the state constitution that a Minnesotan run for the presidency. But the state has set a record in recent history for producing politicians who have received national recognition. Senators William Windom and Cushman K. Davis were considered presidential possibles by many. John A. Johnson was nominated for the presidency in 1908, but he died the next year. Floyd B. Olson, the three-term New Deal governor, was the common first choice to be the running mate of Franklin Roosevelt in 1936, but he also died at the height of his career. Harold Stassen, the "boy governor," vied for the presidency in 1948 and 1952 and a few more times. Humphrey, after his term as Vice President, became his party's presidential candidate in 1968. Divisiveness within the Democratic Party over the Vietnam issue hurt his potential election – a divisiveness that was provoked by Eugene McCarthy, the professor-politician-poet-philosopher, who was Humphrey's political kin in the Minnesota Democratic-Farmer-Labor Party. McCarthy's intellectualism and disdain for hawks garnered a following of disaffected young people. However, neither McCarthy nor his protégés were able to launch an effective campaign. Humphrey and McCarthy were the state's most serious presidential aspirants until Minnesota Senator Walter A. Mondale got into the act. Mondale withdrew his candidacy in 1974 but ran a full-fledged campaign in 1984. Other Minnesotans who have graduated to the national scene are Secretary of Agriculture Orville Freeman and Chief Justices of the U.S. Supreme Court Warren Burger and Harry Blackman.

Humphrey came to the U.S. Senate in 1948 and the whole world noticed that Minnesota was the only state to call a major political party something other than Democratic or Republican. Henry H. Sibley, the state's first governor, was a Democrat but for the next forty years the Republicans reigned. Franklin D. Roosevelt, in 1932, was the first Democratic presidential candidate to win Minnesota's electoral votes. Minnesota's legacy of liberal Republicans began early. Senator Moses Clapp and the famous aviator and congressman Charles Lindbergh led the resurgence against President William Howard Taft's conservatism.

Minnesotans are also pioneers of the choral tradition. Germans and Scandinavians brought their singing societies with them when they settled on the new soil. Before guitars or melodeons were used for accompaniment, they developed a number of first-class capella choirs. The father of choral music was F. Melius Christiansen, a Norwegian musician who directed the St. Olaf College choir for almost forty years. The Northfield choir presented a prototype for choral music as it performed on both coasts of the United States and throughout Europe.

The Minneapolis Symphony Orchestra evolved from choral singing. Emil Oberhoffer, a young Bavarian musician, was engaged to direct the Apollo Male Chorus which began in 1895. Oberhoffer embellished many major works with an orchestral accompaniment, but felt frustrated because of the difficulty in assembling enough musicians for a single performance. A permanent symphonic organization was essential. In November, 1903, Oberhoffer directed the Minneapolis Symphony Orchestra's first concert.

When the orchestra was founded, Minneapolis ranked eighteenth among the United States cities in population, and yet only six other cities maintained their own symphony orchestras. A symphony rarely pays for itself; it depends on a music-loving community like Minneapolis.

Over the years the orchestra's baton has been passed through several hands: there was Henry Verbrugghen, a Belgian; Eugene Normandy, Hungarian, and Dimitri Metropoulis, who was for many years The Maestro. Antal Dorati, a Hungarian like Ormandy, followed Metropoulis. In the fall of 1960 a thirty-six year old Polish Conductor named Stanislaw Skrowaczewski came to direct the Minneapolis Symphony Orchestra. During his reign it became the Minnesota Symphony Orchestra and was given a new home. Private contributions provided nearly all the thirteen-and-a-half million dollars required to build the concert hall, which opened in October 1974. Minnesota's director, Neville Marriner, a native of Lincolnshire, England, is one of the world's most recorded conductors.

For twelve consecutive seasons, American-born Leonard Slatkin left his post as music director of the St. Louis Symphony Orchestra to conduct the Minnesota Orchestra's summer concerts and present a Viennese Sommerfest to complement the well-attended concerts. Peavey Plaza, the terrace outside Orchestra Hall, is transformed into a "marketplatz" for beer, bratwurst and polka dancers. It's the only place in the country where Slatkin works his programming around a festival. When Slatkin was asked if he were to be reported as "not only a first-rate conductor but also a consummate public relations man – would that bother or flatter you?", he answered with his characteristic quickness, "Just as long as you keep them in that order."

Across the river, the new Ordway Music Theater sits on the spot where the St. Paul Auditorium met its demise at the jaws of a crane. The Ordway Theater is a performing arts facility which presents international and national entertainers in the fields of music, drama and dance. The Minnesota Opera, the 100-year-old Schubert Club and the St. Paul Chamber Orchestra are its principal tenants.

In 1980, world-class violinist Pinchas Zukerman stepped on stage to begin his stint as conductor and music director of the St. Paul Chamber Orchestra. It was unusual for him to stand in front of an audience without a violin in his hand. Several people, including his mentor, Isaac Stern, expressed a concern about his diversion from the violin. Zukerman responded, "Look, I was born to create sound. You think I can give it up?"

Zukerman was raised in Tel Aviv and has said that he has not stopped playing the violin since his father handed him a half-sized version in 1955. When Zukerman was seven he had already played and discarded the recorder and clarinet. At the tender age of thirteen he left his family

and came to America. For a short time he bypassed his music and the frustrations of school in a new land, favoring the adventures to be found in a pool hall. "When Isaac Stem found out, he pinned me against a wall," Zukerman once told an interviewer. "He did everything but punch me. He got me to see that music isn't a profession; it's a way of life. I was sixteen. There was still time, thank God."

Twin Citians thank God too. They are grateful that music is on his mind "every minute of my waking life," because it shows in his attitude. When he first arrived in St. Paul he told the players in his orchestra "You play in Bemidji, you play in Carnegie Hall. You give 100 percent wherever you are."

Twin Citians boast of another man who was transplanted to Minneapolis for a period of time. As patrons of the performing arts the cities rank high. But practically all professional theater was still in New York City when Irish director Sir Tyrone Guthrie arrived in Minneapolis in 1959. He was disenchanted with Broadway, judging its producers to be more concerned with the box office than serious theater. Land was donated, civic leaders pledged earnest money, and a corps of 1,200 volunteers fanned out to raise two million dollars to build the facilities. In the decades since, the Guthrie Theater has given the Cities masterful productions of the major classics, with excursions into novel and contemporary theater as well. Broadway star George Grizzard reminisces: "There are three or four things in a twenty-five-year career that stand out for you: *The Adams Chronicles*. The ... production of *Man and Superman* in New York and playing Hamlet at the Guthrie for Tyrone Guthrie."

Together the Minneapolis Institute of Arts, Walker Arts Center, Children's Theater, the Science Museum of Minnesota, the University of Minnesota's Wind and Jazz Ensembles, the Minnesota Opera and the Minnesota Zoological Garden supply the cultural smorgasbord.

The Minneapolis Aquatennial, the biggest summer festival in the United States, lasts for ten days in July. It incorporates more than 200 sports and entertainment activities, highlighted by an evening "Torch Light" parade. The State Fair is a Minnesota institution dating back to 1859. Each year, during its twelve-day run ending on Labor Day, over a million individuals see the state's best-attended annual event. The fair, reported to be the country's largest, is operated by the Minnesota State Agriculture Society. St. Paulites celebrate in the chilling temperatures with their annual ten-day Winter Carnival, which started back in 1886. Now, each January, King Boreas and his Queen of the Snows preside over the International 500 Snowmobile Race, an ice-carving contest, winter golf and softball, ski jumping. A few masochists even go waterskiing – river ice permitting.

Contrary to out-of-state rumors, Minnesotans don't thrive on cold weather; they simply tolerate it. Each of the Twin Cities has an elaborate skyway system which makes it possible to get through a major part of the downtown areas without testing the wind chill factor. The IDS Center, with its beautiful Crystal Court, is near the center of Minneapolis' fourteen-block system of overhead corridors and arcades that connect most of the downtown buildings. St. Paul's system is similar, and both are expanding. The two-towered, twenty-seven-story, seventy-five million dollar Town Square in St. Paul is the site of offices, a major department store, fifty-five shops and a glass-covered park, with underground parking for 500 cars.

The talk of the town in Minneapolis is the restored riverfront where you will find St. Anthony Main, the Nicolet Island Inn, Fuji Ya and Riverplace, with its exciting restaurants, shops and cabarets. The area is set off by the historic charm of cobblestone streets. Minneapolis' fifty-three-story City Center, with its shopping mall, office tower and hotel, is the downtown area's most popular attraction.

St. Paul is especially proud of its refurbished Union Depot, St. Paul Hotel and the Old Federal Courts Building – renamed Landmark Center. Both towns are simultaneously constructing new edifices and preserving those of the past and both towns have worked to provide enjoyment of nature within the city limits.

Minneapolis has an ambitious and extensive riverside project along fifteen miles of the Mississippi. Pigs Eye in St. Paul is one of only two rookeries located in the heart of a big city. This unique wilderness is besieged by the city – a sewage plant, railroad marshaling yards and fleets of barges. But within its boundaries are tall silver maples and cottonwoods, mink, beaver, 226 great blue heron, 1,000 smaller black-crowned night herons and 320 egrets. The wildlife area is named after Pierre 'Pig's Eye' Parrant, a notorious French fur trader and bootlegger. He built the first shack within the boundaries of St. Paul in 1838, after being expelled from Fort Snelling military reservation.

The Twin Cities have long since shaken off the makeshift look of their youth. Together they provide a world for all seasons and though differences do emerge, the spirit of collaboration supersedes that of competition.

Northfield lies nestled in southeastern Minnesota, about fifty miles south of the Twin Cities, in a rolling, tree- and water-filled land. Carleton College is found there, the Midwest's answer to an Ivy-League school. Carleton is a small, academically excellent liberal arts college with a carefully gleaned faculty including academics from far afield and a nationwide student body. To enhance its Eastern ambiance, the place received its name in 1871 from William Carleton of Charlestown, Massachusetts, who had given an unrestricted gift of 50,000 dollars – the largest single gift yet given to a "western" college. Donald Cowling, who took over Carleton's presidency in 1909 and ruled with an "iron fist," had four degrees from Yale. John Nason, the president from 1962 to 1970, was a Carleton graduate, a Rhodes Scholar and a past president of Swarthmore in Pennsylvania. Lawrence Gould, the man who ran Carleton after Cowling and before Nason, was second in command with Admiral Byrd in Antarctica. Carleton College was founded as Northfield College in 1866 by the Minnesota Conference of the Congregational Church. That body was strongly linked to established Congregationalists on the East Coast, whose Puritan philosophy toward superior education caused them to support a mission college on the frontier. The Congregationalists also set up Yale University, Dartmouth, Williams, Amherst, Bowdoin, Middlebury, Oberlin, Knox, Olivet, Beloit, Grinnell, Whitman, Fisk, and others.

Cowling's deftness lay in fund-raising, the hiring and keeping of good people and in recruiting students from coast to coast. Gould led Carleton to national prominence (the median Scholastic Aptitude Test (SAT) score of the student body jumped 135 points during his reign). Still, Carleton did not escape the anti-establishment fallout of the sixties. Atherton Bean, Carleton '31, chairman of the executive committee of the International Multifoods Company, was president of Carleton's board of trustees during the late 1960s. He watched the cyclone of discontent cross the country and warned John Nason to be prepared. The effect of the "Make Love not War" slogan spread. Two or three Carleton men burnt their draft cards and, before long, co-ed housing became a fact of the Northfield school.

Carleton students were active in the Honeywell Project, a protest against fragmentation bombs. Ed Spencer, then president of Honeywell, was invited to campus to answer questions. According to a former student, "He made the mistake of coming." Because of Carleton's first Earth Day, in April 1970, four of their student leaders were interviewed on NBC's *Today Show* and the national press became further aware of concern for this planet's future. Then came the killings at Kent State in Ohio on May 4, 1970. Feeling the impact of that blow, the Carleton students went on strike. There followed an eruption of mass meetings and teach-ins . It wasn't until 1972 that the blaze of demonstrations began to die down.

In 1970 Howard Swearer became Carleton's president. He came from the Ford Foundation and stayed until 1976, when he took up the presidency of Brown University. For the most part he was in charge of a less turbulent group of students. The "me" generation had emerged.

Robert Edwards, who came to Carleton after leading the Middle East and African Program of the Ford Foundation, capitalized on the college's proximity to Minneapolis and St. Paul and, therfore expanded selection of cultural offerings. At the same time, Carleton faculty and students can appreciate the bucolic charms of a rural town. Originally a farm service town, the pastures now meet what has become a college community supplied with concerts, local chamber music groups, bookstores, little theater groups and a superior classical music station provided by St. Olaf College.

Carleton is not the only institution of higher learning in town. On a hill across the way lies St. Olaf, another first-rate college. Carleton has bestowed about 1,000 doctorates, St. Olaf about 900, and Macalester, a venerable college in St. Paul, about 500. Harlan Foss, president of St. Olaf, maintains that two schools in a town are better than one. Their academic departments regularly co-sponsor colloquia and share resources.

St. Olaf and Carleton share the Northfield tradition of Jesse James Days. On September 7, 1867, the Jesse James-Cole Younger gang met stiff resistance at the local bank. Their carefully planned Northwest Bank raid was thwarted by the heroism of Northfield's citizens and particularly the bank teller, Joseph Lee Haywood, who refused to give the outlaws the money. Jesse James and his gang got away, but 100 men were hot on their trail. The event is celebrated annually, the weekend after Labor Day.

A world-famous medical center and a procession of charming river towns lure thousands of visitors to Hiawathaland. Southeast Minnesota is distinctively different from the rest of the state in its topography, its climate and the character of its towns. Rochester, the area's largest city, is just as unique. It is a modern city with progressive social, cultural, recreational and industrial characteristics, but those attributes are obscured by its reputation as the healing capital of the world.

The Mayo Clinic is the largest association of privately practicing physicians on earth; a group many believe represents an unparalleled proficiency in medical diagnosis and treatment. Rochester's visitors, therefore, include people from all parts of the globe. Of the half million people who come to the city each year, at least half are patients of the Mayo Clinic. The number of people seeking the clinic's services is amazing. But 250,000 people come to Rochester for other reasons. That's a lot of visitors for a town of 70,000. Many of visitors stay at the Kahler Hotel. The Kahler takes up nearly a square block in downtown Rochester. Kings of nations and prairie country farmers pass each other in the lobby and share an elevator on the way to their rooms and suites. Some 100,000 guests stay annually. Fifty shops, including three barber shops, a beauty salon, drug store, airline ticket office, travel agency, stockbrokerage, an antique store, a boutique and numerous restaurants are dispersed throughout the hotel.

The Kahler management aims to please its guests and therefore accommodates even rather unusual requests. South Americans like fresh squid, which must be flown in from Chicago. Leo Durocher had a mattress stored for him in a closet and Lyndon Johnson reserved an elevator just for his entourage. Lyndon and Lady Bird stayed in the 205-dollar-a-night J.H. Kahler Suite, where a dozen yellow roses welcomed their arrival. There, Johnson "held court," recalling tales of World War II and the LBJ Ranch to his enraptured audience.

The faces and names of notable guests are recorded in the rows of photographs along "Celebrity Lane." Jack Benny played "Love in Bloom" on his violin when he was at the Kahler Hotel. Eddie Cantor stayed there, and so did a host of other international celebrities from the worlds of sport, cinema, theatre, music and politics, including kings and presidents. For example, Franklin D. and Eleanor Roosevelt stayed at the Kahler, and he was indirectly responsible for Rochester's adoption of a new-fangled invention.

President Franklin D. Roosevelt's visit to Rochester, in 1934, sparked an interest in locating a radio station there. It all began when two Rochester men – Gregory Gentling and Clare Fischer – traveled to Washington D.C. to persuade President Roosevelt to come to a program honoring Drs. William J. and Charles H. Mayo. The sceptics thought the suggestion "preposterous"; the President wouldn't take time to visit that small frontier town.

But Roosevelt did come to Rochester, and so did a cavalcade of newspaper and radio people. Among them was Stanley Hubbard, owner of Radio Station KSTP in the Twin Cities. Hubbard and Gentling talked about the possibility of a radio station serving Rochester and southeastern Minnesota. Convinced it would work, Gentling organized the Southern Broadcasting Co. and the station went on the air in 1935. Soon Rochester's citizens, along with those in St. Paul, Minneapolis and Duluth, could hear: "Who knows what evil lurks in the hearts of men? The shadow knows ....." and, Molly "Heavenly days, McGee!" Fibber: "Dad-rat the dad-ratted ... I gotta straighten out that closet one of these days," and, "A fiery horse with the speed of light, a cloud of dust and a hearty hi-yo Silver!" Amos 'n' Andy, Fred Allen, Jack Benny, Eddie Cantor and Bob Hope joined Fibber McGee and Molly as they helped listeners forget their troubles during the Great Depression.

However, there's more to Rochester than the Mayo Clinic and the celebrities who stay at the Kahler or come on over the air. Rochester has become a substantial industrial base. The biggest boost was provided in 1956 by International Business Machines (IBM) which chose Rochester as the site for a huge manufacturing complex. IBM employs about 4,000 local people – approximately as many as the clinic requires – which is good news for Rochester people. Indeed, IBM was a forceful factor in Rochester's economic growth. Today the city has over seventy manufacturing firms whose combined payroll exceeds fifty million dollars.

The city of Rochester maintains two dozen parks. Mayo Park, with its formal gardens and sculptured memorials to the famous doctors, is a favorite. The Zumbro River winding through town becomes a setting for many summer events, including an annual Festival of the Arts. A short distance north of the downtown area is Silver Lake Park, the site of Rochester's acclaimed movable hallmark. Twenty thousand wild Canadian geese winter there each year and several are year-round residents. Occasionally flocks will take off together and fly in symmetrical V-formations. But for the most part they coast on the water or strut about on the shore, graciously accepting handouts from their appreciative audience.

Rochester is a hospitable town. It has the warmth of a small community and the cosmopolitan feeling of a big city. The per-capita income of its citizens is well above the state and national average, making it a good place to live as well as to visit.

Someone called Rochester "a little town on the edge of nowhere," and so it probably seems to many who have traveled from faraway places to find it. Around it stretches a countryside of well-ordered farms, with round red barns, softly turning windmills and pastures dotted with fat, contented cattle. In southeast Minnesota, thick forests meet rolling hills and meadows, and chortling trout streams meander lazily through the woodlands. It is a place where tiny villages and hamlets have withstood change and where corn and the dairy cow support the economy.

Minnesota is associated with lakes, but this corner of the state is characterized by its beautiful rivers and streams. It is reminiscent of the foothills in parts of the Appalachians or the Ozarks – a land of hills and hollows, of ravines and forested limestone bluffs. Black walnut trees grow in the valleys, and hickory in the hills. Wild turkey and bobwhite quail, possums and huge timber rattlers hide in the woods. Canoeists pass clear, cold springs, caverns and rushing rapids.

Less than half-an-hour from Rochester by car is Mantorville. On the way lie mildly neglected water mills and covered bridges which provide a welcome dose of nostalgia. That short journey takes one through a past century. Mantorville, listed in the National Register of Historic Places, has been maintained and preserved since its inception. As the seat of Dodge County, its courthouse has been in continuous use since 1865. Here, too, the Hubbell House has been standing since 1857, and the once prosperous hotel is now one of Minnesota's oldest and most famous restaurants. During the 1862 Indian Uprising, local people welcomed the protection of its forty-inch-thick limestone walls.

Just west of Mantorville is the town of Wasioja. Today

it is hard to imagine that the village of seventy-five residents was larger than Rochester at one time. That was in the mid-nineteenth century when the town had a population of 1,000 on an important Territorial Road stagecoach stop.

At that time it had a weekly *Wasioja Gazette*, a fairground, a race track, a seminary and many stores and buildings encircled by limestone sidewalks cut from local quarries. One of the general mercantile stores might have sold fence staples, salt blocks and cattle, bridles and harnesses, hardware, stove pipes and dampers, bottled ink, peppermint stick candy, spool thread and needles, traps for both muskrat and mouse, cornhusking hooks, fly swatters, patent medicines, mason jars and lids, lye for soap making, oil cloth and yard goods, candles and kerosene lamps.

But the railroad bypassed Wasioja and the townspeople's plans for prosperity were crushed. Only few homes and landmarks remain. In Wasioja is the only Civil War Recruiting Station to survive in Minnesota. Nearby are the hollowed ruins of a Baptist Seminary. At the outbreak of the Civil War, ninety seminary students marched to the recruiting station to enlist, forming the core of the Minnesota 2nd Regiment, the heroes of Chickamauga. Sadly, no one returned and the seminary closed. A fire in 1905 reduced the building to its present state of ruin.

South of Rochester, the Root River begins its scenic journey east to the Mississippi River, passing Lanesboro, with the state's largest trout hatchery, Preston, Rushford, Houston, Hokah, La Crescent and other communities which contribute to the distinct character of this region. The great glacier that blanketed the rest of Minnesota thousands of years ago missed this portion of the state. A drive through this hill country evokes a feeling of being in New England. The valleys are covered with wild flowers and are excellent for bird watching. You may even spot a bald eagle. At the western tip of the region, Albert Lea's Helmer Myre State Park boasts Big Island on Albert Lea Lake, where 400 species of wild flowers bloom each year. In Austin, the Geo. A. Hormel Co., a meat-packing plant, processed 600 hogs during 1892 but now it can process as many in forty minutes. Hormel is listed in *Fortune* magazine's 500 largest industrial companies. Back at the Mississippi River valley, the region around La Crescent is famous for its apple orchards.

The first major stop up the river valley is Winona. The Hotel, a romantic Victorian inn, is also listed in the National Register of Historic Places. In the 1850s Winona was a first-rate sawmill town, with some 2,000 loggers and 1,500 mill hands at work in ten sawmills. By 1862 Winona had become the fourth largest wheat market in the United States. The Julius C. Wilke, built in 1898 at Rock Island, lies at the shore of the river at the end of Main Street as a reminder of the great steamboat era. In the late 1800s 8,585 steamboats rounded the bend at Winona in one year. Brick-making also became an important industry to Winona. One plant produced three million bricks during the 1920s. The quarries developed from the sandstone bluffs which border the town. The bluffs also provide a magnificent view of the river valley. Sugar Loaf, where the Dakota Indians held sacred ceremonies, is 500 feet high.

Farther upstream is Wabasha, a prototype of a Mississippi River town. The Anderson House, in downtown Wabasha, is Minnesota's oldest operating hotel. "Dutch Kitchens" have been creating savory dishes since 1856. Across the antique bridge is a vast marsh, a major part of which is in the Upper Mississippi Wildlife and Fish Refuge that was established in 1924. These 195,000 acres comprise wooded islands, sandbars, lakes and marshes which stretch from Wabasha to Rock Island, Illinois. Reportedly, the National Wildlife Refuge is home for 270 different species of birds, fifty of mammals, forty-five of amphibians and reptiles and 113 of fish. In late March and in early April you can see 5-10,000 whistling swans in the Weaver Bottoms near Weaver.

Above Wabasha the Mississippi River broadens into Lake Pepin. Sailboats, barges, cruisers and motorboats carrying fishermen are scattered on the twenty-one-mile long, one-and-seven-tenths-miles-wide lake. It was here, in 1922, that eighteen-year-old Ralph Samuelson tied eight-foot pine boards to his feet and was pulled behind a motor boat; the world's first water skier lived in Lake City. This town, which made buttons from river clams in the 1900s, lies at the edge of Lake Pepin. Nearby Red Wing was "the greatest primary wheat market in the world" in 1871. More recently it was better known for its pottery. Today, the renovated St. James Hotel is most often associated with the river town that was founded by the Sioux Indians, who chose a scarlet-stained swan's wing for their emblem of their chiefs, hence the town's name. Charles Biederman, renowned for his primary-colored geometric abstractions, lived in Red Wing.

The southwestern portion of Minnesota has been labeled Pioneerland. Several historic sites are found in this area, through which the Minnesota flows: near Granite Falls lie granite boulders, which are approximately 3,800,000,000 years old; in Cottonwood County, the Jeffers Petroglyphs, ancient Indian carvings are found, and at Fort Ripley, the ruins of a major battle in the Sioux Uprising of 1862 remain as part of the state's heritage. Southwestern Minnesota has its share of ethnic festivals too. A Czechoslovakian kolacky, or fruit-filled bun, the cause of Montgomery's annual Kolacky Days, and New Ulm's German Heritagefest offers a variety of festivities. To embellish the Eastern European flavor of the region, the Schumachers have restored a hotel in New Prague which was built in 1898 by Cass Gilbert, architect of the Minnesota State Capitol, the U.S. Custom House, the Woolworth Building in New York, and the U.S. Supreme Court Building in Washington D.C. Schumacher's New Prague Hotel resembles a Bavarian country inn. Hand painted Bavarian folk art decorates the restaurants and twelve rooms, which are named for the months. Each room has coordinated design, colors and accessories. Small prints, antiques and custom-made furniture painted with Bavarian roses, Austrian linens, Persian rugs, tapestry hangings and Bavarian lamps can be found in several of the rooms. The menu, with about fifty-five main dishes, is strictly Czechoslovakian fare.

Pipestone Quarry in southwestern Minnesota is associated with some of the region's earliest history. When the first explorers and fur traders reached the area, they found it peopled largely by two divergent Indian tribes – the Dakota Sioux and the Objibwa. The quarry, which provided the Indians with stone to make their calumets, or peace pipes, was already ancient and became

Minnesota's first national monument in 1937. Today it is unquestionably the state's most popular Indian site.

Minnesotans may have forgotten that years ago Henry W. Longfellow referred specifically to that spot in his *Song of Hiawatha* in the following lines:

> On the Mountains of the Prairie
> On the great Red Pipestone Quarry,
> Gitche Manito, the mighty,
> He the Master of Life, descending,
> On the red crags of the quarry
> Stood erect and called the nations,
> Called the tribes of men together.

In reality, Longfellow never saw the country. His mountains are the Coteau des Prairies. Though we wouldn't think of calling them mountains, many of the explorers used that term in their narratives. Coteau des Prairies, named by French explorers, means Highland of the Prairies. The elevation of land was formed by the ice sheet of the last glacial epoch and is the terminal moraine left by one of the massive nodes of this great ice mass. The "coteau," or highland, begins in the eastern Dakotas and continues southeastwards into Iowa. The slope begins and ends so gradually as to be almost imperceptible. In Pipestone County, stone outcroppings interrupt that gentle decline. It is in this quarry country that the government established an Indian Reservation, then an Indian school and, finally, a national monument. Understandably, it is the Indians themselves who accorded the land the most regard. To them it was *wakan* or sacred.

The pre-Columbian Indian had a Stone Age culture. He lived close to nature, but in no way was he its master. He lived in awe of his surroundings and worshipped the sun, moon, waterfalls, fire, rocks. Because superstition invaded his spiritual feelings, he sought to appease the spirits to fend off evil which would otherwise be inflicted upon him.

It follows that the Indian would be impressed by the mysterious, ethereal character of rising smoke. Because the practice of smoking was widespread among the tribes, the pipe and tobacco became common accoutrements at ceremonial gatherings. A type of pipe, named calumet by the French, was used most often. The bowl of the calumet, in which the tobacco was placed, was shaped from a hard substance, generally stone. Attached to the bowl was a hollow, two- to three-feet-long stem. The calumet seems to have been revered for centuries. It was used to make treaties more binding, to put strangers into the category of friends, to insure safe passage through country held by other tribes and to promote peace.

Ceremonial pipes used by the Plains' Indians came in considerable quantities from Minnesota. While some of the native Americans went directly to the quarry, others obtained their calumets through trade.

East of Pipestone, at Jeffers, is one of the oldest messages in Minnesota. It was carved in a rock by an Indian about 5,000 years ago and is a picture of an *atlatl*, a spear-throwing instrument similar to the harpoon used by Eskimos later. Beginning in about 3,000 B.C., Indians used pointed rocks to peck symbols in a twenty-three-mile-long outcrop of rock. Many people from different tribes carved the pictures over a span of time up to 1750 A.D. Though large numbers were destroyed, over 2,000 of the Jeffers "petroglyphs" (rock pictures) still exist. There are carvings of bear, elk, bison, turtles, wolves, bows and arrows, medicine men, dragonflies, stick men and several carvings which defy description. Some anthropologists believe that the nondescript designs are ancient doodles. Some carvings are more than three feet across; others are only a few inches.

From about 3,000 B.C. to 500 A.D., big game animals provided most of the Indians' food. The huge bison (a now extinct ancestor of today's buffalo) was the most coveted. Small bands of hunters followed the migrating bison herds and drove them over cliffs or into narrow ravines. The Indians would then kill them with their spears and *atlatls*.

Perhaps as many as 125 million buffalo grazed the grasslands of the United States in the seventeenth century. The Dakota Indians have described enormous clouds of frost that could be seen on the horizon; the belled breath of buffalo herds often twenty miles wide. These people discarded no part of their kill. Tails became fly swatters, stomachs made serviceable canteens and ribs were made into runners for sleds. White men, however, killed tens of millions of the animals in the latter part of the eighteenth century, wanting only their skins and tongues – the gastronomic delicacy of that era. Tongues of buffalo were claimed to have filled entire riverboats. By 1900, the herds of millions had dwindled to just 300 wild and 969 domesticated animals. A small herd of their descendants is still found in Blue Mounds Park State Park. Original plant life of the prairie such as prickly pear, buffalo grass and cacti grow in Blue Mounds Park today, which is located in the southwest corner of Minnesota.

Just east of the Blue Mounds Park is Worthington, the state's turkey capital. For thirty-six years the big birds have strutted down main street on King Turkey Day, unaware that at the end of the 150-yard trail they'll be prepared for Thanksgiving dinners.

The Dakota Indians, defeated by the Objibwa in the game-rich north, fled to these plains where the buffalo roamed through six feet tall grass. Settlers began filtering into the region by the mid-1800s, transforming the plain into rich farmland, battling against winter storms, famine, grasshopper plagues and loneliness. In *Giants in the Earth*, O.E. Rölvaag, Governor Karl F. Rölvaag's father and former teacher at St. Olaf, gives us a vivid picture of the struggles and triumphs of the first people to occupy the plains of Southern Minnesota:

"BRIGHT, clear sky over a plain so wide that the rim of the heavens cut down on it around the entire horizon.

"... And sun! ... It set the heavens afire every morning; it grew with the day to quivering golden light – then softened into shades of red and purple as evening fell ... Pure color everywhere ... Now and then a dead black wave would race over the scene ... a cloud's gliding shadow ... now and then ...

"It was late afternoon. A small caravan was pushing its way through the tall grass. The track that it left behind was like the wake of a boat – except that instead of widening out it closed in again.

"'Tish-ah!' said the grass ... 'Tish-ah, tish-ah! ... Never had it said anything else – never would it say anything else. It bent resiliently under the tramping feet; it did not break, but it complained aloud every time – for nothing like this had ever happened to it before ... 'Tish-ah, tish-ah!' it cried, and rose up in surprise to look at this rough, hard thing that had crushed it to the ground so rudely and then moved on.

"A stocky, broad-shouldered man walked at the head of the caravan. He seemed shorter than he really was because of the tall grass around him and the broad-brimmed hat of coarse straw which he wore. A few steps behind him followed a boy of about nine years of age. The boy's blond hair was clearly marked against his brown, sunburnt neck; but the man's hair and neck were of exactly the same shade of brown. From the looks of these two, and still more from their gait, it was easy to guess that here walked father and son.

"Behind them a team of oxen jogged along; the oxen were drawing a vehicle which once upon a time might have been a wagon, but which now, on account of its many and grave infirmities, ought long since to have been consigned to the scrap heap ... Over the wagon box long willows saplings had been bent ... On these arches were spread two hand-woven blankets that might have adorned the walls of some manor house in the olden times. On top of the blankets were thrown two sheepskin robes ... which were used for bed coverings at night.

"Hitched to this wagon and trailing behind was another vehicle, homemade and very curious-looking ... It too was a wagon, after a fashion ... Both wagons creaked and groaned loudly every time they bounced over a tussock or hove out of a hollow ... 'Squeak, squeak!' said the one ... 'Squeak, squeak!' answered the other ... The strident sound broke the silence of centuries.

"A short distance behind the wagons followed a brindle cow ... She had been jogging along all day, swinging and switching her tail, the rudder of the caravan. Soon it would be night, and then her part of the work would come – to furnish milk for the evening porridge ...

"Across the front end of the box on the first wagon lay a rough piece of plank. On the right side of this plank sat a woman with a white kerchief over her head, driving the oxen. Against her thigh rested the blond head of a little girl, who was stretched out on the plank and sleeping sweetly. Now and then the hand of the mother moved across the child's face to chase off the mosquitoes which had begun to gather as the sun lowered ... beyond the girl, sat a boy about seven years old – a well-grown lad, his skin deeply tanned, a certain clever, watchful gleam in his eye. With hands folded over one knee he looked straight ahead.

"This was the caravan of Per Hansa who, with his family and all his earthly possessions, was moving west from Fillmore County, Minnesota, to Dakota Territory. There he intended to take up land and build himself a home; he was going to do something remarkable out there which should become known far and wide. No lack of opportunity in that country, he had been told! ... Per Hansa himself strode ahead and laid out the course; the boy Ole, or Olamand, followed closely after ... The cow Rosie trailed behind, swinging and switching her tail ...

"'Tish-ah, tish-ah!' cried the grass ... 'Tish-ah, tish-ah!'

"The caravan seemed a miserably frail and Lilliputian thing as it crept over the boundless prairie toward the skyline ... The whole train – Per Hansa with his wife and children, the oxen, the wagons, the cow, and all – might just as well have dropped out of the sky ... (the caravan) steered for Sunset Land! ... for more than three weeks now ... Early in the journey it had passed through Blue Earth; it had pushed westward – always westward ... Strange that he hadn't reached Split Rock Creek before this time!

"On they went, farther out toward Sunset Land – farther into the deep glow of evening ...

"The mother had taken little Anna up into her lap and was now leaning backwards as much as she could; it gave such relief to her tired muscles. The caresses of the child and her lively chatter made her forget for a moment her care and anxiety, and that vague sense of unknown which bore in on them so strongly from all directions ... Ole sat there and drove like a full-grown man ... Out on the skyline the huge plain now began to swell and rise ...

"The afternoon breeze lulled and finally dropped off altogether. The sun, whose golden lustre had faded imperceptibly into a reddish hue, shone now with a dull light, yet strong and clear; in a short while, deeper tones of violet began to creep across the red. The great ball grew enormous; it retreated farther and farther into the empty reaches of the western sky; then it sank suddenly ... The spell of evening quickly crowded in and laid hold of them all; the oxen wagged their ears; Rosie lifted her voice in a long moo which died out slowly in the great stillness. At the moment when the sun closed his eye, the vastness of the plain seemed to rise up on every hand – and suddenly the landscape had grown desolate; something bleak and cold had come into the silence, filling it with terror ... Behind them, along the way they had come, the plain lay dark green and lifeless, under the gathering shadow of the dim, purple sky ...

"Suddenly she could stand it no longer. She ran over to him, flung her arms around his neck, and leaned close against him. The dam of her pent-up tears broke in a flood of emotion; she wept long and bitterly.

"'Now calm yourself, dear ... You must calm yourself, Beret-girl!' ... He had put his arm lovingly around her, but found it hard to speak."

Silence enshrouded that curve of empty land until, one by one, caravans crossed it. "How exciting they were those little ships of the Great Plain! ... rigged with canvas tops which gleamed whitely in the shimmering light ... Many queer races and costumes were to be seen in these caravans ... every last one of them was in high spirits, though they knew no other home than the wagon and the blue skies above ... The Lord only could tell whence all these people had come and whither they were going!"

"And it was as if nothing affected people in those days ... everything was possible out there. There was no such thing as the impossible any more. The human race has not known such faith and such self-confidence since history began."

Minnesotans can't duplicate those circumstances, but they have inherited the optimistic and industrious spirit of their forefathers. Perhaps it is the sharp contrasts of four overindulgent seasons. Whatever the reasons the lessons that were learned on that prairie have endured.

Left and overleaf: Ash River and (previous page, above and top left) the town of Island View on the far banks of Rainy Lake in Voyageurs National Park (these pages), northeastern Minnesota. This park backs onto the Canadian border, covering an area networked with water channels leading from Lake Superior to the Lake of the Woods. It was dedicated in 1975 to preserve the remaining wilderness and commemorate those early voyageurs, the French-Canadian trappers, who were the vanguard of the seventeenth, eighteenth- and nineteenth-century fur trade. Rainy Lake is one of the three biggest of the thirty major lakes within a park riddled with waterways.

At one point it was estimated that one in every nine Minnesotans lived in a place overlooking water, whether a lake or a river. It seems natural, then, that water skiing should have been invented in Minnesota, and that Birch Lake (left), in Bear Island State Forest, should have motor boats drawn up at intervals along its shore. The state has an irresistible attraction for water sport enthusiasts nationwide. In a state so rich in Indian history and place-names, one can hardly help wondering how those early inhabitants would have described the reeds swirling under the surface of Robinson Lake (overleaf). Perhaps they would have seen them as the tresses of a lovelorn Indian maiden who had drowned herself in the lake, or the fingers of a river spirit . . . .

If there were any doubt that Minnesota is a bonafide Great Lakes State, its 180 miles of Lake Superior shoreline would dispel those doubts — and besides, Minnesota contains 15,290 other lakes — including the source of the great Mississippi River, Lake Itasca. The taupe-streaked sky of evening and the platinum light playing on Lake Superior give credence to the state's old Dakota name, mnísóta, which means white water.

Split Rock Lighthouse (facing page), in Split Rock Lighthouse State Park (these pages and overleaf), rises up over the North Shore of Lake Superior. The North Shore is often tempestuous and, at Split Rock, magnetic interference makes compasses all but useless. During its sixty years of service, the lighthouse beam was a lifeline for vulnerable seafarers.

Precariously perched and fragile-looking harebells (facing page top) grow on the often windblasted and rocky shore of Lake Superior at Grand Marais (these pages). As well as being rich in scenery, this area gives up gems to eager-eyed visitors; jasper, agate, lintonite and thompsonite are all to be found along the beaches of Lake Superior.

The burning ball of evening's sinking sun throws the lighthouse (facing page) at Grand Marais (these pages) on Lake Superior into black relief and highlights the lake with molten color, slinging gold over Grand Marais Lake (above). In such quiet conditions the coast guard (top) seems redundant. Among the famous tourists to love Grand Marais were Babe Ruth and Jack Dempsey, who used to spend time at a private resort nearby.

The Temperance River (right and overleaf) gushes between tree-lined banks through Superior National Forest, where the winter trees look like slender white spears. It runs from Temperance River State Park on Lake Superior to Sawbill Lake.

The Baptism River (right) flows through some beautiful scenery within Baptism River State Park, which is now incorporated in Tettegouche State Park. Remaining pictures: Lake Superior near the point where the Baptism River flows into it.

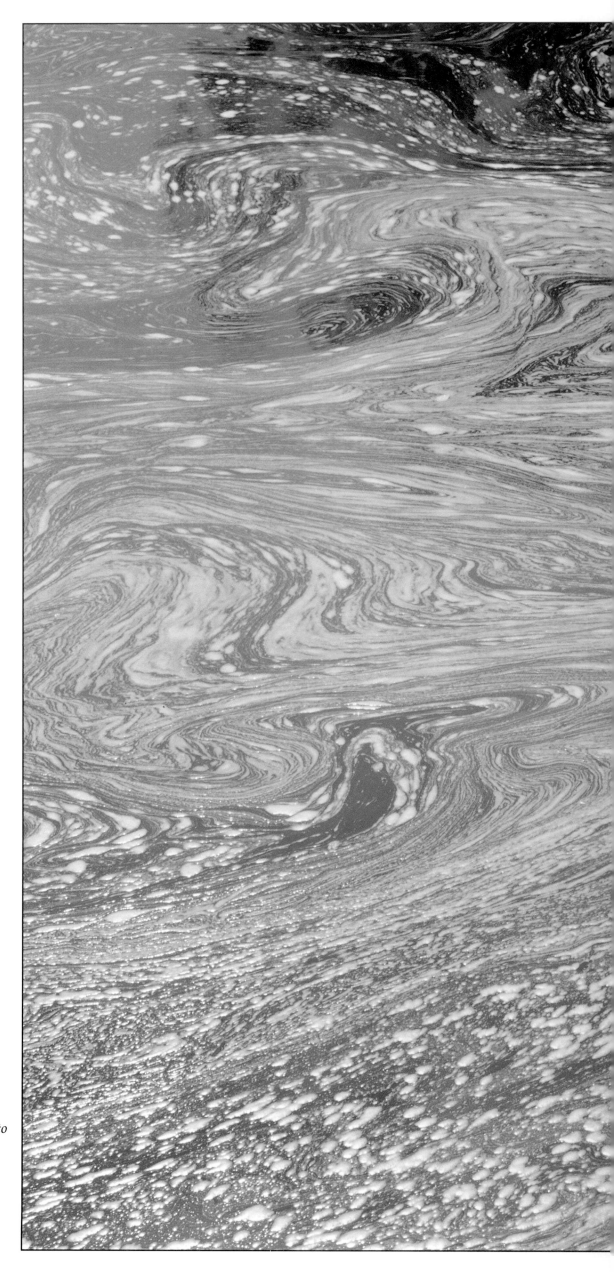

The Baptism River (right and overleaf), its swirling lines as intricate as any in a Chinese painting, flows through Finland State Forest into Lake Superior.

The Baptism River (these pages), in its quieter moments, provides excellent fishing for brook and brown trout.

The Beaver River froths up dangerously to white water before it careers over steep drops on its course.

The Gooseberry Falls (these pages) are found in Gooseberry Falls State Park, one of Minnesota's most beautiful. Here the Gooseberry River hurtles over a sheer drop of more than 100 feet, crashing in a cascade of frothing spray.

Above, top and overleaf: rapids on the bubbling Gooseberry River, leading to the spectacular Gooseberry Falls. The Gooseberry River (facing page) meanders through Gooseberry Falls State Park.

The Knife River, near Two Harbors, looks placid and still, as if it is hardly moving at all but simply holding a mirror up to the sky.

Above: Hill City Lake, to the west of Duluth, and (right and top right) the shores of Lake Superior, viewed from Hartman Park. Duluth was named for Daniel de Greysolon, Sieur du Luth, after his arrival here in 1679. Daniel de Greysolon established a fur-trading post not far from Duluth after conference with the Chippewa Indians of the area and then moved on toward Mille Lacs, claiming territory for France. His is one of the earliest recorded visits of a European to Minnesota. This state was the last of the great Midwestern states to be settled. In fact, a great many of the settlements on the shores of Lake Superior were not established until the 1950s.

The view from Duluth (these pages) is an inspiring one of Lake Superior lying beyond Duluth Harbor (above and top left). Duluth is the world's largest inland port and connects Minnesota to the Atlantic Ocean via the St. Lawrence Seaway. Despite its importance to shipping, lunker pikes in excess of twenty pounds have been caught in this harbor, along with brown trout, coho and chinook salmon from Lake Superior. Left: Glensheen, London Road – the restored thirty-nine-room Jacobean-style manor built for Chester Congdon, attorney, mining entrepreneur and state legislator. Much of the original furniture is still in place, and the house's decorative details include handcarved woodwork, marble fireplaces and fittings made of alabaster, brass, silver, ivory and art glass.

The aerial lift bridge spanning the ship canal at the entrance to Duluth Harbor is a landmark of the area. It was based on a bridge in Rouen, France, and built by the engineer Thomas F. McGibray between 1901 and 1905. Powered by a battery-operated motor, its roadway can rise to a clearance of 130 feet in sixty seconds.

As well as being a commercial port, Duluth Harbor (these pages) has plenty of room for smaller fishing and leisure boats.

WEGMANN CABIN

It was here, in 1900, that Theodore Wegmann and his wife Johanna built a log cabin and a log storpool office. Here they welcomed tourists to newly-created Itasca State Park with mitch and lodging. Here Wegmann carried out his duties as the first park game warden - a job he held for 25 years. Here, in the later years of his life, he sad and looked out at the lake he loved and told stories of early Itasca. Here in the park's Pioneer Cemetery Wegmann and his wife are buried.

The building presently standing was the storepool office. The duplicate log building was built in 1977 to demonstrate pioneer log cabin construction.

Left: Wegmann Cabin in Itasca State Park (top left), northwestern Minnesota, where the
Mississippi River has its source in Lake Itasca. This area of Minnesota is known as Vikingland
because evidence found around Alexandria suggests that it may have been visited by Norsemen
more than 100 years before the arrival of Columbus. Above: a secluded inlet on Lake Bemidji,
Beltrami County, in the Heartland – home of Paul Bunyan, Charles A. Lindbergh and Sinclair
Lewis. Bald and golden eagles nest in the wetlands of Tamarac National Wildlife Refuge (overleaf).

Left and overleaf: Bass Lake near Grand Rapids, which began life as a lumbering town. This is perhaps the sort of scenery with which Bob Dylan would have been familiar. His home town, Hibbing, lies to the northeast of Grand Rapids.

Right and top right: Deer Lake, north of Grand Rapids, and (above and overleaf) Pughole Lake, hemmed about with birch and pine and strewn with water lilies.

Kremer Lake is the sort of vision that could spur a city commuter into poetry. Its flowering reeds and placid reflection of an indigo sky would soothe the most agitated spirit.

The waters of Lake Winnibigoshish (these pages) have invaded the pine forest at West Seelye Bay (top right), where pink lady's thumb and water lilies grow. There is evidence to suggest that the lake area has been inhabited since its formation through the glacial retreat, over 10,000 years ago.

Ten Mile Lake Lutheran Church in Dalton.

Above and right: Leech Lake in Chippewa National Forest, part of a reservation for Chippewa or Ojibwa Indians. Island Lake (top right), in Becker County, is inclined to overflow its bounds, flooding parts of the surrounding forest (overleaf).

Above: wind-ruffled fields of grain and sunflowers gild the Dunvilla countryside, and arable land around Fergus Falls (right and top right), in Otter Tail County, shows just how rich this state's farmland can be. This is the sort of Minnesota scene associated with a famous past resident, Laura Ingalls Wilder, to whom the sight of waving grain and fertile farmland would have been very familiar. The state is renowned for its agricultural output, particularly of corn and oats.

The distant towers of Minneapolis rise above Lake Calhoun, which, despite its proximity to this major metropolis, is a bass fisherman's joy.

The tall, dark IDS Tower, built in 1972, dominates downtown Minneapolis (these pages) and is part of an urban design incorporating the Crystal Court and skyway system, in which it is possible to shop, see a show and eat without having to set foot outdoors – handy for winters in which the temperature has been known to reach -41°F.

The Foshay (facing page) and IDS (above) towers loom over Peavey Plaza, Minneapolis (these pages). Overleaf: 3rd Avenue Bridge over the upper lock of the St. Anthony Falls. These falls were named in 1680 by the Belgian priest Father Louis Hennepin for his patron saint. He came across the future site of Minneapolis while he was a prisoner of the Sioux.

The august governmental institutions of the
Twin Cities, for example Minneapolis' City Hall
(right) on Government Center Plaza, have
produced several very well known politicians,
including Walter Mondale, Hubert Humphrey
and Eugene McCarthy.

*The Foshay Tower (facing page), overlooking Peavey Plaza (facing page bottom), was Minneapolis'
first skyscraper, built in 1929. For years this 447-foot-high building was the tallest in the
Midwest, and it received international attention when, in 1981, a huge yellow ribbon was tied
around it to welcome back American hostages from Iran. Above: the classical-style Federal Office
Building, Minneapolis (these pages).*

Built between 1896 and 1903, the Saint Paul State Capitol Building (these pages) was designed by
Cass Gilbert, who won the commission in a competition and produced a beautiful Beaux-Arts,
Classical-style building with a large, unsupported marble dome. The gilt statue on the front of the
building, entitled "The Progress of State," is the work of Daniel Chester French and Edward
Potter. Overleaf: the House Chamber of the State Capitol Building.

The Robert Street Bridge (right), Saint Paul (these pages), crosses the Mississippi River parallel to the Wabasha Bridge, which traverses Navy Island (top right). It is hard to believe that this graceful city, full of Art Deco and Victorian architecture, this town where F. Scott Fitzgerald drank in the elegant Commodore Hotel, was once called Pig's Eye. But it was. In 1839, the commandant of Fort Snelling evicted a former fur trader called Pierre "Pig's Eye" Parrant for selling whiskey to the Indians. So Pig's Eye and his friends moved downstream, eventually forming a straggling collection of log cabins euphoniously named Pig's Eye Landing. It was a French priest, Father Lucien Galtier, who requested that the village's name be changed in favor of the saint to whom he had dedicated the small log chapel he had built there.

The Cathedral of Saint Paul (left), designed by Emmanuel L. Masqueray, is constructed partly from Saint Cloud granite, which is famous for its beautiful color variations of pink, red and gray. The cathedral owes something to Spanish Renaissance, Italian and classical styles as well as to its main inspiration, St. Peter's in Rome. The Landmark Center (above), originally the Old Federal Courts Building in Saint Paul (these pages), dates from 1901 – although building began in 1894. It is built in the style known as Richardsonian Romanesque, and the south tower is modeled after Trinity Church in Boston.

Saint Paul has definitely been a river town ever since the first riverboat docked at Fort Snelling in 1823. The Mississippi winds itself in a huge loop through the city, giving Saint Paul twenty-nine miles of riverfront and confusing anyone trying to determine their north/south position in the city using the river. The prows of riverboats (right) still plough the river, but these days more usual river traffic consists of tugs and grain-laden barges.

Meighen Store (top left), in Forestville State Park, is all that is left of a once thriving little town in this wooded valley. In 1910, Thomas J. Meighen locked the door of what had been the supply center of Forestville since 1858 for the last time. The railroad had passed the town by forty-two years earlier, in 1868, perhaps making its demise inevitable. But before it finally lost the competition for settlers and business, Forestville had boasted three mills, two hotels, two stores, a furniture factory, a wagon shop and a tavern. Lock and dam No. 5 (left) on the Mississippi (above) is part of the state's system of dams and locks, which extends along the Mississippi River from the Twin Cities to the point where it flows out of Minnesota and forms the border between Iowa and Wisconsin.

The Julius C. Wilkie Steamboat Center at Winona is a full-scale replica of an old-time steamboat. Winona stands at the foot of massive limestone cliffs that rise 500 feet above the river and is named after an Indian woman called We-No-Nah, who threw herself over these cliffs, distraught that her intended marriage to the brave she loved had been thwarted. The city's river-town character is celebrated in the week of July 4 with a Steamboat Days Festival.

JULIUS C. WILKIE STEAMBOAT CENTER
ON THIS SITE THE ORIGINAL OLD WOODEN HULL STERNWHEELER,
THE JULIUS C. WILKIE WAS ENSHRINED FROM 1956 TO 1981,
WHEN IT WAS DESTROYED BY FIRE. IT WAS SO NAMED IN HONOR OF
A WINONA PIONEER MACHINIST AND INVENTOR. THROUGH THE
VISION AND GENEROSITY OF THE WILKIE FAMILY AND THE
DETERMINED EFFORTS OF THE ENTIRE WINONA COMMUNITY, THIS
JULIUS C. WILKIE STEAMBOAT CENTER HAS ARISEN FROM THE ASHES.
CHRISTENED JULY 3, 1982
MANUFACTURED AND DONATED BY THE WINONA MONUMENT COMPANY

Top right: farm buildings near Redwood Falls, and (right) arable land around St. George. Above: the Mississippi River near Red Wing. The name Red Wing comes from Koo-poo-hoo-sha, the title given to Dakota Indian chiefs who once ruled the area. It meant "wing of the wild swan dyed scarlet" and referred to their symbol of leadership.

Fireweed grows in Frontenac State Park (left) over the area which was once home to the Dakota and Fox Indians. The park's Havana Ridge Site shows archaeological traces of an ancient settlement dating from 400 B.C. Overleaf: Whitewater State Park.

INDEX

Baptism River 49, 50, 51, 52, 53, 54, 55
Bass Lake 78, 79, 80, 81
Beaver River 56, 57
Birch Lake, Bear Island State Forest 30, 31
Deer Lake 83
Duluth 68, 69, 70, 71, 72, 73
    Aerial Lift Bridge 70, 71
    Duluth Harbor 68, 69, 70, 71, 72, 73
    Glensheen 68
Frontenac State Park 126, 127
Gooseberry Falls 58, 59
Gooseberry River 58, 59, 60, 61, 62, 63
Grand Marais 40, 41, 42, 43
    Grand Marais Lake 42
    Grand Marais Lighthouse 43
Hartman Park 67
Hill City Lake 66
Island Lake 93, 94, 95
Wegmann Cabin, Itasca State Park 74
Julius C. Wilkie Steamboat Center, Winona 122, 123
Knife River 64, 65
Kremer Lake 86, 87
Lake Bemidji 75
Lake Superior 34, 35, 37, 40, 41, 42, 43, 48, 49, 67, 69
Lake Winnibigoshish 88, 89
Leech Lake, Chippewa National Forest 92, 93
Meighen Store, Forestville State Park 120
Minneapolis 98, 99, 100, 101, 102, 103, 104, 105, 106,
    107, 108, 109

City Hall 106, 107
Federal Office Building 108
Foshay Tower 102, 109
Government Center Plaza 106, 107
IDS Tower 103
Lake Calhoun 98, 99
Peavey Plaza 103, 109
St. Anthony Falls 104, 105
Third Avenue Bridge 104, 105
Mississippi River 100, 101, 104, 105, 114, 115,
    120, 121, 123, 124
Pughole Lake 82, 83, 84
Robinson Lake 32, 33
Saint Paul 110 – 119
    Cathedral of Saint Paul 116
    Landmark Center 117
    Navy Island 115
    Robert Street Bridge 115
    State Capitol Building 110, 111, 112, 113
Split Rock Lighthouse State Park 36, 37, 38, 39
    Split Rock Lighthouse 37
Taramac National Wildlife Refuge 76, 77
Temperance River 44, 45, 46, 47
Ten Mile Lake Lutheran Church, Dalton 90, 91
Voyageurs National Park 25, 26, 27, 28
    Ash River 26, 27, 28
    Island View 25, 26, 27
    Rainy Lake 25, 26, 27
Whitewater State Park 128